GOTHIC SERPENT

Black Hawk Down
Mogadishu 1993

CLAYTON K.S. CHUN

ACKNOWLEDGMENTS

I would like to thank several individuals who supported me in writing this
monograph. Many of my colleagues at the US Army War College gave me a
big hand in the project. Colonel Pat Cassidy supplied many photographs
from his deployment to Somalia. Colonel Mike Mara also provided much
information about his assignment as an AC-130 pilot supporting UNOSOM
II, and gave his observations about Somalia. Colonel Tom Sexton ran down
several reports from SOCOM. I would also like to thank my editor Phil Smith
from Osprey for encouraging me to complete this project. My most sincere
thanks go to my family for sacrificing their time to allow me to complete
this work.

GLOSSARY

AFSOC	Air Force Special Operations Command
AIAI	Al-Ittihad al Islami
APC	armored personnel carrier
AWSS	authorized weapons storage site
C2	command and control
CAP	combat air patrol
CCP	casualty collection point
CENTCOM	US Central Command
CIA	Central Intelligence Agency
CISE	CENTCOM Intelligence Support Element
CSAR	combat search-and-rescue
FLIR	forward-looking infrared
HUMINI	human intelligence
HMMWV	High Mobility Multipurpose Wheeled Vehicle
IR	infrared
IV	intravenous
J-2	intelligence staff (under a joint organization)
J-3	operations staff (under a joint organization)
JCS	Joint Chiefs of Staff
JSOFOR	Joint Special Operations Forces-Somalia
JTF	joint task force
JOC	joint operations center
JSOC	Joint Special Operations Command
LAW	light antitank weapons
NGO	non-governmental organization
LAW	light anti-tank weapon
NSC	National Security Council
QRF	quick-reaction force
RPG	rocket-propelled grenade
SAW	squad automatic weapon
SNA	Somali National Alliance
SOAR	Special Operations Aviation Regiment
SEAL	Sea, Air, Land (US Navy SOF)
SOCOM	US Special Operations Command
SOF	special operations forces
TF	task force
TFR	Task Force Ranger
TOW	tube-launched, optically tracked, wire command data linked guided missile
UNITAF	United Task Force
UN	United Nations
UNOSOM	United Nations in Somalia
USAF	US Air Force
USC	United Somali Congress

CONTENTS

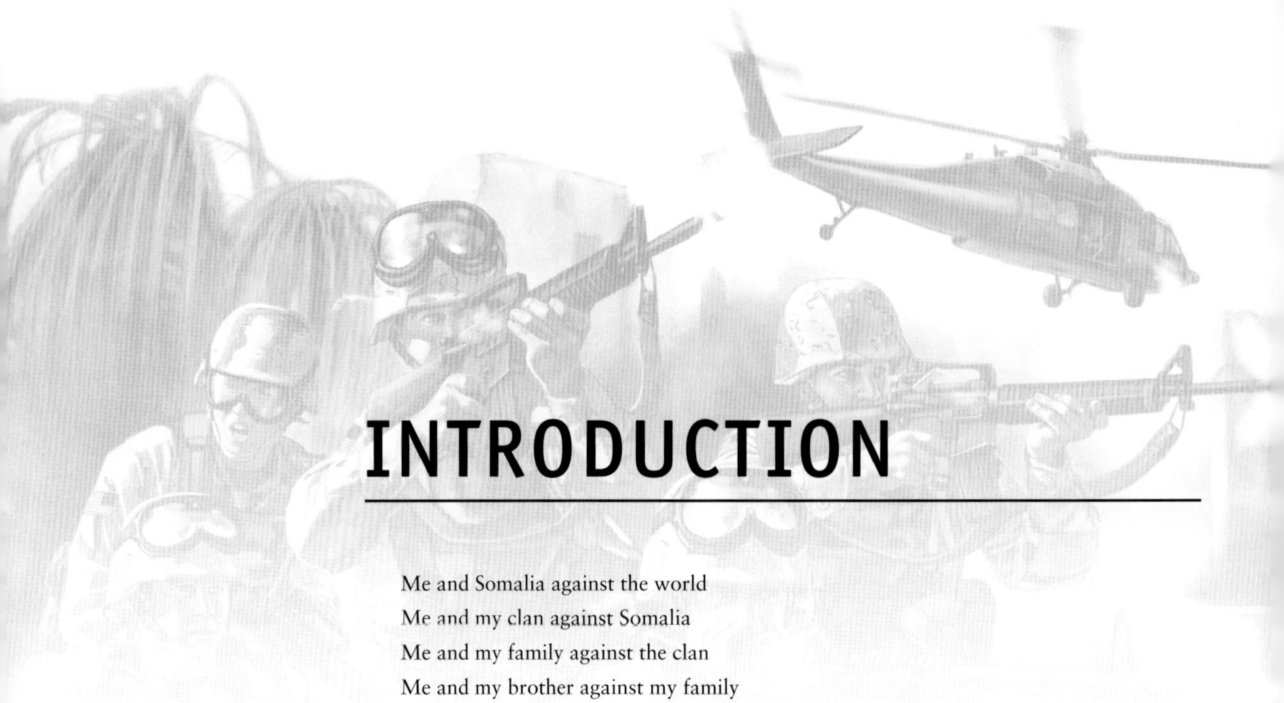

INTRODUCTION

Me and Somalia against the world
Me and my clan against Somalia
Me and my family against the clan
Me and my brother against my family
Me against my brother.

Somali Proverb

In 1992, the United States basked in the glow of its recent military and political victory in Iraq. Washington had successfully orchestrated a coalition of nations, including Arabic states, to liberate Kuwait from Saddam Hussein. The US administration was also celebrating the fall of the Soviet Union and the bright future of President George H.W. Bush's "New World Order." The fear of a nuclear catastrophe seemed remote given the international growth of democracy. With the United States now as the sole global superpower, some in the US government felt that it now had the opportunity, will, and capability to reshape the world by creating democratic states around the globe. The only concern for some was where to start, given the many areas that would merit rebuilding. Africa was hardly on Washington's list of vital national interests. Somalia was a remote failed state created from Italian and British colonies. Although bordering the Red Sea and the Indian Ocean, the region had been a minor focus of the Cold War. Moscow supported regimes first in Somalia and later in Ethiopia. Few Americans knew or cared about Eastern Africa. Other areas seemed more important.

Somalia was a country that had fallen into chaos. The country had suffered a devastating civil war when various factions overthrew its dictator, Mohamed Siad Barre. Barre, who came to power in late 1969, had tried to build a socialist state by subverting historic clan allegiances. Barre's strong-arm methods worked as he outlawed political parties and clans. Mogadishu received military aid from the Soviet Union to advance his rule – Somalia offered Moscow an African foothold and a major naval port on the Indian Ocean. However, Barre fell out of Soviet favor when he attacked neighboring Ethiopia. As a new socialist state,

JANUARY 26
1991

Barre's Somalian
dictatorship
overthrown

4

SOMALIA: CLANS AND ISLAMIC TERRORISTS

Supporting UN operations is a tough mission for combatants and non-combatants alike; it was even harder without a single government entity with which to negotiate, so the UN and Washington had to interact with clan and tribal leaders. Somalia was a patchwork of clans artificially formed into a country. During its colonial period from the late 19th to mid 20th centuries, Somalia fell under the rule or control of various foreign powers including the Italians, French, and British. African neighbors, such as the Ethiopians and Kenyans, also governed areas along with ethnic Somalis. The situation changed with the end of colonial rule and the formation of the Republic of Somalia in 1960. Various governments ran Somalia until Mohamed Siad Barre's reign, but despite his administration's control of the Somali government and its people, Barre had a very difficult time handling the clans and their activities.

As Somalia descended into chaos, the only unifying force was the clans. Somali clans dictated how their members lived, who got food, and which members could earn a living. Here, a Somali clan representative hands out work permits. (DoD)

Somalis share a common culture, but differ through clan association. Somalia's Dir, Isaaq, Darood, Hawiye, Digl, and Rahanwein clans make up the largest groups in the region. Barre came from the Darood clan, while his rival Mohamed Farrah Aideed claimed roots in the Hawiye. Under the clan system, members show allegiance first to family, then to their clan, and finally the nation. The major clan groups had sub-clans that further divided Somalia. Rulers, whether they were Barre or Aideed, had to satisfy clan needs first at the expense of other clans or the national interests. Political patronage and favoritism brought inevitable conflict. Squabbles over resources, political power, or other issues divided Somalia. Control over the clans and Somalia could only come with authoritarian rule and force under Barre. For Barre, the banning of clans under his regime, while giving the appearance of favoring his clan, further alienated the government from the Somali people and helped lead to a civil war.

Internal strife after Barre's fall led to a rise in insurgencies fuelled by clans and other groups. Somalia's civil war brought opportunities for many non-clan groups to expand their activities, while the nation's collapsed economy led to arms smuggling and *khat* drug trafficking. The social breakdown also brought poverty and willing converts ready to fight. With no central authority to fear, terrorist organizations made their home in Somalia in the early 1990s, with the goal of creating a Somali government following Islamic laws, since almost all Somalis are practicing Muslims. One group, the Al-Ittihad al Islami (AIAI), offered aid and fighters to rebels in the Ogaden area. The AIAI wanted to help these rebels to break away from Ethiopia and extend their radical Islamic message; Osama bin Laden, according to American intelligence sources, had links with the AIAI.

Aideed's propaganda claims that the UN and Americans were trying to convert the Somalis away from Islam played on the people's Muslim beliefs, regardless of clan affiliation. It also helped extended the influence of radical Islam. The struggle between an Islamic people and the Americans may have brought another party into the conflict, with serious future implications. Allegedly, the Somali National Alliance (SNA) militia, who opposed Task Force Ranger (TFR) soldiers, trained under al-Qaeda and the AIAI. Many of the al-Qaeda members who trained the SNA had served in Afghanistan against the Soviets and now the Americans in Somalia. Ironically, American intelligence agencies may have armed and trained some of the same radical Islamic fighters in Afghanistan who would eventually help shoot down two American helicopters and cause Washington to pull out of Somalia.

President George H.W. Bush, late in his administration, committed the United States to humanitarian relief efforts in Somalia. Massive famine in Somalia motivated him to send the military to support the UN. (Col Pat Cassidy)

Ethiopia had offered further expansion into Africa for the Soviets. The Soviet government therefore cut off aid and support to Somalia, and Washington furthered the schism between Moscow and Mogadishu when it came to Barre's side.

Destroying Somali clan associations and activities was impossible. There were six major clans with 20 sub-clans in Somalia. The Somali clan leadership felt marginalized and isolated by Barre, hence the clans formed rebel groups against the Barre government, supported by Ethiopian arms and aid. One clan, the Hawiye, started a political movement, the United Somali Congress (USC), in defiance of Barre. Based in Mogadishu, Mohamed Farrah Aideed headed the USC. Aideed, a former general in Barre's regime, came from one of the largest and most powerful Somali clans, the Habr Gidr, a sub-clan of the Hawiye. In an effort to crush Aideed in Mogadishu, Somalia's capital, Barre started to crack down on this clan, but Aideed became a warlord with control over a large part of Mogadishu. Unfortunately, Barre's efforts turned violent and resulted in several massacres. Washington turned off its aid to the Somali government. The nation exploded into civil war and chaos, and Aideed and other rebel groups overthrew Barre on January 26, 1991. Disorder immediately followed.

The Bush administration had been wary about an African deployment. There were no appreciable national interests in eastern Africa, other than humanitarian. Without the threat from the Soviet Union and competition for proxy states, Washington's desire to engage with the continent ended. Yet disturbing images from Somalia caught the President's attention. Drought, civil war, and clan violence heightened Barre's fall and the power vacuum that followed. There was no replacement government in Somalia and the nation fell into chaos. Despite creating a country from the two colonies, Somalia suffered from poverty. Once political agreement and law enforcement fell apart, clan fighting turned the state into a lawless region controlled by warlords like Aideed.

Fighting, poor agricultural output, and a breakdown of Somalia's economy contributed to famine, and soon the world press began showing starving Somalis on screen and in print. Non-governmental organizations (NGOs) tried to distribute food, but continued clan fighting over control of aid distribution forced calls for more security. The United Nations (UN) reacted to the worsening food situation. In April 1992, under UN Resolution 751, a 550-man Pakistani security contingent arrived in Somalia to support distribution of $20 million in food aid. Under the UN Operation in Somalia (UNOSOM), a Pakistani force tried to quell some of the food-distribution problems caused by rival clans, but it failed. By August, the peacekeeping force expanded to

Mogadishu did not have a functioning government. This is a typical urban scene in the city. American military personnel had to provide basic services, like medical and dental aid, to the population during Operation *Restore Hope*. Somalis lived a tenuous daily existence among the clans with uncertain food and medical aid. (DoD)

3,500 personnel, but the humanitarian aid campaign continued to flounder. UN officials wanted security operations to include the possibility of disarming the clans.

Somalia fell into anarchy, and clan members robbed food aid workers to resell the aid and strengthen their grip over the population. UNOSOM peacekeepers did not have the weapons, support, or force size to maintain order. Bush finally acted and he pushed for American involvement to stop the suffering. Advisors cautioned that this effort would require massive aid and a military deployment – other areas also called for more attention from Washington, like the conflict and ethnic cleansing in the Balkans. Still, Bush was transfixed on Somalia. The US Air Force (USAF), under Operation *Provide Relief*, logged 2,500 flights out of Mombasa, Kenya, delivering 28,000 tons of food. No American military members served as peacekeepers, yet. Despite the massive aerial relief effort, food aid was limited, but if the UN could control a major port, then it could send in vast supplies. This proposal, however, would require a large increase in military forces to ensure security, especially around cities like Mogadishu. The only nation that could accomplish this effort in size and scope was the United States.

Washington's involvement would evolve from a famine relief action into combat operations. The US military leadership became wary of the mission expanding from feeding the starving to trying to police a lawless Somalia. There seemed to be no defined political objectives for the Americans, other than stopping clan warfare. While the UN wanted to rebuild Somalia into a viable state, there was confusion in Washington about how much support to provide to the UN. This situation would change for the United States after a small raid in Mogadishu on a Sunday afternoon in October 1993.

APRIL 1992

First UN operation begins in Somalia

ORIGINS

Public and UN pressure mounted on the White House to do more for Somalia. In Washington, the National Security Council (NSC) met on four occasions from November 20 to 26, 1992, to consider several options. NSC alternative plans ranged from providing only logistical support to sending an American-led and US-dominated force to oversee the mission. In Somalia, deaths due to starvation and warlord violence mounted – analysts estimated that 300,000 people died, mostly women and children. America's commitment to world stability and the media's attention on starving Somalis convinced Bush to expand the US commitment. Providing humanitarian aid in Somalia seemed more palatable than engaging in UN and NATO peacekeeping efforts against ethnic cleansing in Bosnia. Still, some American officials urged caution. National Security Adviser Brent Scowcroft agreed that getting into Somalia would be easy, but cautioned that getting out might be difficult. Chairman of the Joint Chiefs of Staff (JCS)

Despite the presence of peacekeepers, violence and corruption plagued UN food distribution. Clans claimed control over the food, and thereby enhanced their reign over their territory and people. The increased deployment of UN forces threatened the clans' access to this food aid. (DoD)

General Colin Powell saw no other option but to use massive force to end the suffering, but he raised issues about entering a civil war.

With two months remaining in office, Bush approved a plan to send a sizeable American force to support the UN, named Operation *Restore Hope*. The proposal went to UN Secretary General Boutros Boutros-Ghali for approval. Some nations objected to a perceived American influence, which would change the humanitarian nature of the mission. They feared a significant increase in military force structure might make the clans feel threatened and cause additional fighting. Boutros-Ghali had no alternative but to accept Bush's offer, as the UN forces on the ground badly needed security.

**JUNE 5
1992**

Aideed supporters attack UN personnel

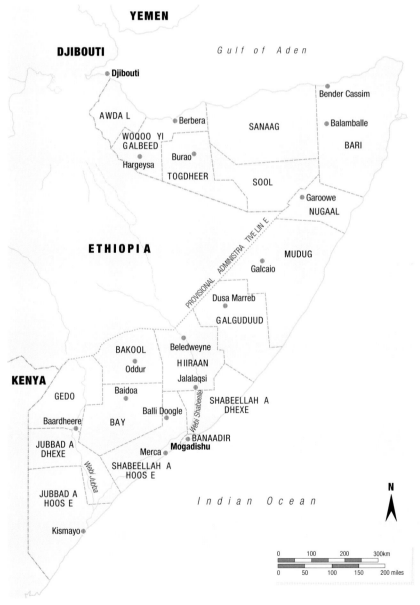

Somalia, 1993

9

The UN's United Task Force (UNITAF) had more than 39,000 personnel. US Marine Corps (USMC) Lieutenant General Robert B. Johnston became the top military commander, with control over American and other UN member forces. US units, organized under Joint Task Force (JTF) Somalia, fell under the US Central Command (CENTCOM), and Johnston controlled the 1st Marine Division and the Army's 10th Mountain Division.

Washington had about 28,900 personnel in Somalia. Their mission included keeping routes opened for relief supplies, securing air and sea ports, providing security for relief efforts, and assisting UN/NGO humanitarian operations. Combining diplomatic efforts with a massive military presence and humanitarian relief did help quiet and pacify the clans. Washington sought to secure areas in Somalia and then turn responsibility over to the UN.

Clans go to War

Somali clans, especially Aideed's Habr Gidr, detested the UN. Aideed harbored a personal hatred for Boutros-Ghali, as the UN Secretary General had supported the Barre regime when he was the Egyptian Foreign Minister. Aideed and others started to challenge UNITAF and fights between clans arose. Ali Mahdi Mohamed, one of Aideed's bitterest rivals in Mogadishu, from the Abgal sub-clan of the Hawiye, sought control of the capital. Both clans clashed in the streets. The United States tried a new tactic to restore order, using Ambassador Robert Oakley to negotiate a ceasefire among the Somali factions. Combined with Johnston's JTF Somalia, the clans seemed outmatched and they agreed to a tentative ceasefire.

Boutros-Ghali wanted a permanent solution through clan disarmament. CENTCOM commander Marine Corps General Joseph Hoar disagreed. This effort would entail a widening of the JTF Somalia mission. Creating secure areas worked because of a tenuous peace between UNITAF and the clans. A source of power and money evaporated from the clans when open robbery of the food relief and other crimes ceased, largely through UNITAF's presence – illegal arms sales, food distribution control, and the *khat* narcotic trafficking provided most of the clans' economic activities. However, any efforts to disarm the warrior-dominated clans would mean war. UN officials deferred a fight when they brokered a deal for the clans to secure their weapons in a cantonment area or authorized weapons storage sites (AWSS). Still, American military forces started to sweep areas for clan weapons, despite efforts to create a Somali police force to conduct these and other operations. Unfortunately, the Somali police were undertrained, ill-equipped, and overwhelmed by the clans. The United States was stuck; the mission had expanded to stabilizing a region where no one could tell who was a foe.

Despite the clans' acceptance of the AWSS facilities, weapons were readily available to any Somali. Firearms were a part of Somalia's warrior culture, in which protection of family and clan was an integral part of life. Violent clashes between clans continued. One incident, in Kismayo, between a clan loyal to Barre and an Aideed ally, occurred on January 24, 1993. UN officials charged Barre's son-in-law, General Said Hersi Morgan, with violating the ceasefire and told him to leave the city. After Morgan

General Joseph Hoar, CENTCOM commander, controlled the Americans assigned both to the UNOSOM and UNITAF missions, and later TFR. Hoar was originally against the use of SOF under TFR in Somalia. (DoD)

refused to depart, UNITAF forces destroyed some of his weapons, including four howitzers, several vehicles, and six trucks mounting recoilless rifles, machine guns, or other weapons, known by the Somalis as "technicals." He returned later on February 22 to attack Kismayo and Aideed supporters, but the effort failed when Belgians and American units forced both sides to disengage.

Unfortunately for UNITAF, major political damage occurred. Aideed had received some false reports that the UN forces had sided with Morgan and the ceasefire and UN peacekeeping efforts had eroded Habr Gidr power. Local officials started to displace the clans in cities. Aideed's anger swelled and he took action.

On February 24, violence spread to Mogadishu. The Habr Gidr clan mobilized to demonstrate against the UN and American presence. The US embassy and UN peacekeepers became targets. Protestors did little damage to the embassy, but over the course of the day Aideed supporters wounded several US Marines and killed two Somali policemen. The fighting continued the next day. American, Nigerian, and Botswanan peacekeepers had to quell protests in Mogadishu. Although the protests were relatively small, the media played up the problems.

The UN versus Aideed

The UN had created some stability in Somalia: a ceasefire had occurred and food distribution continued. Washington now wanted to transfer the major peacekeeping effort to the UN, but the situation changed. President Bill Clinton replaced Bush in January 1993 and he inherited the situation in Somalia. UNOSOM transitioned to UNOSOM II. The UN mission now shifted from humanitarian actions to combat operations under Boutros-Ghali, as clan disarmament became a primary objective to enforce peace. UNOSOM II's military mission was to conduct "operations to consolidate, expand, and

AUGUST 15 1992

US SOF begin supporting food shipments

JUNE 6
1993

UN Security
Council
authorizes action
against Aideed

maintain a secure environment." Under Turkish Lieutenant General Çevik Bir, 28,000 soldiers tried to secure cities, prevent and respond to fighting, control and confiscate weapons, and protect UN activities and personnel. US Army Major General Thomas Montgomery served as Bir's deputy. Montgomery was also commander of US Forces Somalia, with a separate chain of command to CENTCOM, to allay fears of Americans being solely under UN control. About 1,300 men of the US Army's 10th Mountain Division became a quick-reaction force (QRF) to respond to any problems that exceeded the UN force's capabilities, including search and attack missions. USAF AC-130H Spectre gunships based in Kenya provided overhead support.

Despite US/UN efforts to try to rebuild Somalia, the clans were skeptical. Aideed believed the UN helped his rivals. During some AWSS inspections on June 5, Aideed followers attacked Pakistani soldiers. Aideed's supporters had warned that if the UN insisted on AWSS inspections, this activity would translate to a war declaration. Aideed was also concerned that the UN inspections might discover "Radio Aideed," a major propaganda outlet near the AWSS locations. On their return to base, UN Pakistani inspectors faced large crowds on the 21 October Road and, hiding behind women and children, Habr Gidr militiamen ambushed the UN personnel. Another attack occurred at a feeding site on June 5, where the mob killed 23 Pakistanis and Aideed followers captured six more – one died in captivity. The inspectors found evidence of missing technicals and large stocks of TOW (tube-launched, optically tracked, wire command data linked guided) missiles, and other weapons. Boutros-Ghali and other international leaders were livid. Aideed had effectively declared war on UNOSOM II.

On June 6, UN Security Council Resolution 837 was passed. This resolution directed UNSOM II personnel to take all necessary measures against those responsible for the previous day's attack. UN forces conducted tactical operations to arrest Aideed followers, while AC-130s hammered weapon storage areas. UN patrols tried to disarm Somalis, and clan militias responded by ambushing UN patrols, mining roads, and setting up blockades. As a result, the UN posted a $25,000 reward on Aideed.

On July 12, UN forces struck the Abdi House, where members of the

The US Marines conducted several raids to capture weapons from Somali warlords. Here, Marines search a cantonment area controlled by Aideed's clan in northern Mogadishu. These building-to-building searches had mixed results. (DoD)

Lieutenant General Çevik Bir took command of UNOSOM II. The split command relationships between the UN forces and Americans would affect military activities. Although informed of American operations, Bir did not have a say in all activities in Mogadishu involving Americans. (DoD)

USC and Somali National Alliance (SNA) were meeting. The SNA was a political group supportive of Aideed. Intelligence reports indicated the house was a place where Aideed planned his operations, so QRF and American AH-1F and OH-58 helicopters launched a coordinated assault to decapitate the SNA. The AH-1s fired 16 TOWs, and Black Hawk helicopters and trucks delivered troops into the area. The Americans struck the SNA hard. The International Red Cross estimated 54 Somalis killed, but the SNA claimed 74 dead, one of whom was an SNA *imam*. SNA followers also argued that the meeting was developing a plan for an overture to UN peace discussions. In revenge, SNA militiamen killed four reporters who arrived after the attack. This raid ended any possibility of a political settlement.

The US Marines provided security for the early humanitarian efforts in Somalia. UNITAF assets had to deal with clan warfare while protecting a number of UN activities to help starving Somalis and bring the country back from the brink of disaster. Here, Marines secure illegal arms and munitions taken in the Bakara Market area that would have armed clan militiamen. (DoD)

INITIAL STRATEGY

The new Clinton administration believed that it could create democratic states with its extensive diplomatic, economic, and military power. Many believed that only America had the resources to conduct such an effort, and that US power would overwhelm any rag-tag Somali clan. Still, American military muscle was unable to capture Aideed or stop clan fighting and the increasing attacks on UN personnel. Some in the UN and Washington believed the Somali issue required drastic efforts. American ambassador Jonathan T. Howe, a retired Navy admiral, had taken over from Oakley. Desperate to get Aideed, Boutros-Ghali wanted America to deploy its special operations forces (SOF), which had proven their worth in earlier UNOSOM activities. Howe was concerned about escalating the peacekeeping mission to war, but he also advocated using SOF to broaden his options. He turned more toward a military solution than a political one. Secretary of State Madeline Albright and National Security Adviser Anthony Lake also wanted to end the problems caused by Aideed. Powell and Hoar opposed the use of these forces; Powell thought disarming the Somalis was impossible, and Hoar doubted the UN could succeed in Mogadishu. Secretary of Defense Les Aspin also urged caution. Aspin wanted to leave Somalia, since the deployment tied up forces in a long-term mission in an era of declining defense budgets. Clinton administration officials argued for a diminished US role in Somalia and a larger role for the UN. The QRF was smaller than the American logistical support to UNOSOM II, so SOF could possibly get Aideed and keep the US presence low at the same time.

Aideed believed that his existence was at stake, for the UN had now declared war

on him publicly. Increasing UN security, disarmament actions, and the transfer of power to local officials translated into a loss of Aideed's livelihood. Boutros-Ghali and Howe had put a price on Aideed, but unfortunately for the UN, declaring a reward and passing a resolution aimed solely at Aideed had forewarned the clan leader. Strategic surprise was lost and Aideed, who had previously been a visible presence in Mogadishu, went underground. UN and CENTCOM analysts had a difficult time getting information and intelligence on his whereabouts. Trying to capture the Habr Gidr leader would now require credible inside information. Perhaps the only viable course to capture Aideed was through unconventional means.

Task Force Ranger Forms

UNOSOM II forces still patrolled the streets around Mogadishu to maintain a presence and keep an eye on clan activity. The SNA militiamen became the main threat. On August 8, SNA members attacked an American military police patrol – four Americans died in a remote-controlled explosion. This event changed the entire situation for Powell, Hoar, and Aspin. Montgomery, the main American field commander, along with Howe, requested SOF action. As casualties mounted, Powell softened his opposition and supported Montgomery's request to Aspin for SOF.

CENTCOM had anticipated additional SOF deployment to Somalia. The Joint Special Operations Command (JSOC), a sub-command of US Special Operations Command (SOCOM), had started observing and studying Somalia in May 1993. JSOC staff members proposed that a small force of 50 Delta special operations commandos go to Mogadishu. The Delta Force, formed in 1977, seemed perfect for the deployment, since they had a counter-terrorism mission. These commandos prepared to fly on a single C-141 to Somalia on June 5 under Operation *Caustic Brimstone*. However, the force was too small for the mission, and SOCOM proposed a new action.

JSOC intelligence (J-2) and operations (J-3) staffs conducted an initial assessment in Mogadishu from June 12 to 24. The assessment team worked with UN and CENTCOM intelligence sources and also American human intelligence (HUMINT) assets, who were trying especially hard to break into the closed clan structure. Central Intelligence Agency (CIA) assets in Mogadishu had the overall responsibility to track down and report on Aideed.

While in Somalia, the assessment team experimented with ways to get Aideed. JSOC personnel, along with Marines from the American embassy, rehearsed missions – ironically, while US troops were conducting one practice mission, Aideed passed through the exercise area in a convoy, but the assessment team had no authority to capture him. A second assessment team from J-2 visited Mogadishu on July 3. The team found the CENTCOM Intelligence Support Element (CISE) supporting Americans in Somalia and the UN had little experience conducting, coordinating, or analyzing counterintelligence and HUMINT. This limited capability might explain previous

JUNE 7 1993

AC-130H Spectre gunships deployed against Aideed

This AC-130H deployed to Mombasa, Kenya, to aid UNOSOM II forces to search for Aideed after the June 5, 1993, deaths of 24 Pakistani UN peacekeepers. Somalis feared the AC-130Hs due to the aircraft's firepower. The AC-130Hs would later leave Somalia to reduce the American presence. (Col Mike Marra)

One of the most important missions for American military members assigned to Somalia was to protect food convoys from bandits and clan members. Marines from the 2nd Platoon, C Company, 3rd Light Assault Infantry Battalion escort this UN aid convoy traveling from Mogadishu to Biadoa. (DoD)

problems in locating Aideed. CISE personnel came from detached manpower on temporary duty from units around the world, and unfortunately when UNITAF transitioned to UNOSOM II, CENTCOM replaced all CISE personnel. Notwithstanding these structural issues, the J-2 assessment team did think there was a chance of success, a limited one.

The JSOC staff developed three force-structure options for Somali operations, each differing in numbers of personnel and equipment. The largest or "Cadillac" option included a sizeable force with AC-130Hs. The Somalis particularly feared the AC-130s, since they could operate at night and in all weather conditions to deliver 20mm, 40mm, and 105mm howitzer gunfire. The USAF AC-130s had withdrawn to Aviano Air Base, Italy, however, to downsize the American commitment in Somalia. The other alternatives were a medium force ("Oldsmobile") and a small group ("Volkswagen") of about 400 personnel. None of the options included armor. SOCOM sent the alternatives to CENTCOM then to the JCS and to Aspin.

Aspin directed SOCOM to provide forces to Somalia under the Task Force Ranger (TFR) unit. He selected "Volkswagen," since it kept the force at a low level. Despite reservations, Powell agreed, and when briefed Clinton made no objections. The rationale behind the TFR deployment emphasized Somalia's continued lawlessness, increased attacks on UN personnel and installations, and Aideed's hostile acts, all of which strained aid operations. An advanced TFR command element deployed from Fort Bragg, North Carolina, on August 22 and arrived the next day in Mogadishu. On August 25, the main TFR body of about 400 personnel was sent to Somalia. TFR elements included C Squadron Delta Force, 3rd Battalion, 75th Ranger Regiment, and the 1st Battalion, 160th Special Operations Aviation Regiment (SOAR). The 160th SOAR operated MH-60L Black Hawks and AH-6J and MH-6 Little Bird helicopters. MH-60Ls and MH-6s provided transport capability for TFR, while the AH-6s gave a very valuable attack capability, especially at night. Additionally, TFR had US Navy Sea, Air, Land (SEAL) Team Six members and USAF pararescue and combat controllers. By August 28, TFR consisted of 441 personnel.

TFR's deployment created some issues with command relationships. Montgomery did not have command of TFR, which was led by Major General William F. Garrison, whose chain of command bypassed Bir and the UN. Garrison was responsible to Hoar only. He would coordinate with Montgomery, but did not require his approval for a mission. TFR did coordinate operations to reduce conflicts over airspace, avoid disrupting UN activities, and warn Montgomery of actions, however, and although self-contained, TFR might require the 10th Mountain's QRF.

Garrison's orders from CENTCOM changed over time. TFR's initial mission under Operation *Gothic Serpent* was to deploy SOF to support

UNOSOM II. The specific CENTCOM mission statement was to "capture General Aideed and/or designated others, and turn over captives to United Nations forces." The mission would later expand on September 8 to include capturing Aideed's lieutenants and targeting his key infrastructure, and it included authorization to "neutralize the critical Aideed" command-and-control nodes. TFR's mission was to break the SNA leadership.

A Study in Contrasts: US/UN Forces and the SNA

TFR seemed like the perfect solution for Somalia. The Rangers, Delta Force, and other TFR members were some of the best-trained and -equipped soldiers in the American military. SOF had an aura of invincibility through succeeding in previous difficult missions. Personnel wanting to become a member of these units had to undergo a rigorous selection and development process. Delta soldiers, however, had more senior and experienced members than the Rangers – many of the Rangers had just entered the military, but they had passed through hard training and were now in Somalia.

TFR came to Somalia at the pinnacle of America's position in the world. Since the end of the Cold War, Washington had tried to reduce defense spending to provide a "peace dividend" to fund other national priorities. Despite the reduction in manpower, equipment, and shutting of bases around the globe, the United States still maintained an ability to send a large military force worldwide. In an era where Washington had to respond to a host of challenges – from strategic nuclear deterrence to military advisement – the United States looked toward conducting more, but limited, expeditionary actions. The government did not want to create any long-term commitments. TFR and the 10th Mountain Division provided the capability to find Aideed and help the UN, then disengage.

TFR had several advantages that it could exploit. Garrison had access to advanced equipment and weaponry. Helicopters, radio communications, night-vision systems, signals intelligence, and other capabilities served as counterweights to the large Somali numbers. These technologies allowed Garrison to conduct operations with the speed necessary to surprise the Somalis. Despite its small size, TFR could deliver precision firepower rapidly throughout Mogadishu. Delta was especially proficient in night operations, which heightened their effectiveness against the Somalis. TFR's speed, surprise, and firepower seemed to outweigh any risks taken to capture Aideed or his lieutenants. TFR was also unencumbered with dealing with the UN, as Garrison only needed approval from CENTCOM to conduct an operation.

TFR worked in secrecy compared to the UN and QRF. American operatives alleged that UN members had made covert deals with Aideed to avoid attacking their UNOSOM forces. For example, some in TFR claimed Italian UN

The Navy's EP-3E provided a valuable service to American military operations in Mogadishu. Its sensors gave American officials important surveillance data and real-time video to watch actions as they unfolded in Mogadishu. The EP-3E was a modified anti-submarine warfare aircraft. (DoD)

Task Force Ranger (TFR) Organization

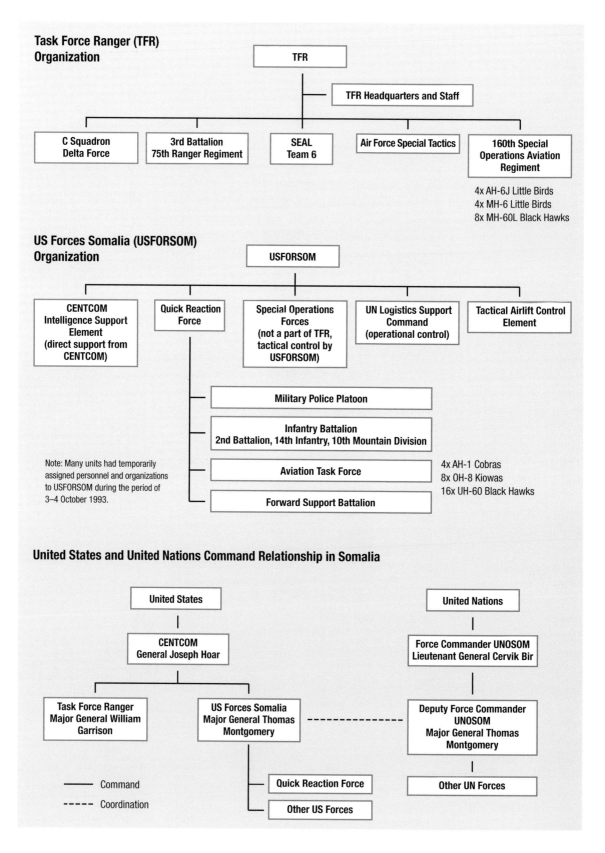

TFR

TFR Headquarters and Staff

C Squadron Delta Force

3rd Battalion 75th Ranger Regiment

SEAL Team 6

Air Force Special Tactics

160th Special Operations Aviation Regiment

4x AH-6J Little Birds
4x MH-6 Little Birds
8x MH-60L Black Hawks

US Forces Somalia (USFORSOM) Organization

USFORSOM

CENTCOM Intelligence Support Element (direct support from CENTCOM)

Quick Reaction Force

Special Operations Forces (not a part of TFR, tactical control by USFORSOM)

UN Logistics Support Command (operational control)

Tactical Airlift Control Element

Military Police Platoon

Infantry Battalion 2nd Battalion, 14th Infantry, 10th Mountain Division

Note: Many units had temporarily assigned personnel and organizations to USFORSOM during the period of 3–4 October 1993.

Aviation Task Force

4x AH-1 Cobras
8x OH-8 Kiowas
16x UH-60 Black Hawks

Forward Support Battalion

United States and United Nations Command Relationship in Somalia

United States

United Nations

CENTCOM General Joseph Hoar

Force Commander UNOSOM Lieutenant General Cervik Bir

Task Force Ranger Major General William Garrison

US Forces Somalia Major General Thomas Montgomery

Deputy Force Commander UNOSOM Major General Thomas Montgomery

Quick Reaction Force

Other UN Forces

Other US Forces

——— Command
- - - - - Coordination

members would signal Somali observers, using vehicle headlights, when TFR was ready to launch a mission from their base at the Mogadishu airport. In addition, Rangers escorting an American intelligence officer to the Italian embassy claimed that they had seen Aideed leave the embassy. Whether these allegations were true or not, the nature of SOF and the desire for secrecy forced TFR to become more independent of the UN and Montgomery.

TFR had some other issues. The split chain of command led to Montgomery's QRF and UNOSOM II forces being deprived of detailed information about TFR operations, but Garrison did coordinate his actions, albeit without much warning. Since Garrison reported to Hoar directly, unity of command was another issue. Montgomery was Bir's deputy in a UN command structure. Montgomery could not task Garrison nor could Garrison directly command the QRF and other UN forces. In case of a problem, TFR might not get adequate and timely reinforcement or support. Similarly, dependency on secrecy also limited intelligence-sharing among forces. TFR could rely on signals intelligence, aerial surveillance by helicopters and EP-3E aircraft, satellites, and ground patrols. The only problem was HUMINT. Breaking into tightly controlled clans and getting precise information on Aideed's whereabouts, especially while he stayed underground, was difficult.

The TFR's component organizations had impressive firepower. The Ranger battalion had three companies; commanders considered the specialized Rangers to be light infantry just like the QRF, and both were similarly organized and equipped. Each Ranger company had three rifle platoons and one weapons platoon. The main firepower that the Rangers brought to TFR was the rifle platoon, which had three rifle squads and a single machine-gun squad. The main armament for the typical Ranger was a 5.56mm M16A2 rifle. Some TFR members carried a CAR-15, a modified M16. The squad also had two grenadiers with M203 grenade launchers.

The New Port provided the UN with an entry point for shipping large amounts of food aid into Mogadishu. The port was also the location where QRF and TFR forces left with UN vehicles to rescue Americans from the Super 61 location. (Col Mike Marra)

19

US military personnel, throughout their deployments in Somalia, set up living quarters throughout Mogadishu. TFR used this abandoned aircraft hangar at the Mogadishu International Airport as barracks and for other activities. The aircraft in the background is from Somali Airlines. (DoD)

The M203 could provide direct fire support with 20 high-explosive grenades, marking smoke rounds, illumination shells, and tear gas munitions. The grenadiers were very important, since they could mark targets with red smoke for spotting by attack helicopters and other elements. A squad also had a 5.56mm, 200-round magazine, M249 squad automatic weapon (SAW). A SAW gunner gave his squad leader the capability to suppress enemy positions or destroy soft targets. The machine-gun squad had three 7.62mm M60s to support the rifle squad and general support.

The rifle squad also carried a variety of hand grenades, including concussion and fragmentation types. Plastic concussion grenades, filled with plastic pellets, allowed a soldier to stun a foe when entering a room or area – they were not lethal munitions. Many Rangers carried these concussion grenades and "flash-bangs" to surprise Somalis upon checking buildings, and fragmentation grenades were used to more destructive effect. American soldiers also had M72A2 light anti-tank weapons (LAWs). There were no active SNA or Somali tanks or armored vehicles, but the LAWs gave an ability to destroy some hardened targets, like a building, or make a hole in a wall.

Delta and SOF members used a combination of weapons. Some used standard M16A2 or CAR-15 rifles. Others used sniper rifles, the GAU-5 (an Air Force aircrew version of the M16), the M14, and other small arms, depending on their mission or preference.

American ground vehicles consisted of High Mobility Multipurpose Wheeled Vehicles (HMMWVs) and two types of trucks. The HMMWV is a light four-wheel-drive tactical vehicle. This 1¼-ton vehicle can serve as a transport or cargo vehicle, ambulance, or armament carrier. TFR HMMWV operators manned M2 .50cal machine guns or operated a Mk 19 40mm grenade launcher. The Mk 19 was especially effective in delivering fire support against enemy personnel or destroying unarmored vehicles. Grenades had a 16ft expected casualty radius against personnel. These grenade launchers were also useful for breaching unreinforced concrete, a common building material in Mogadishu, and they suppressed enemy fire. TFR and the QRF could call upon 2½-ton and 5-ton trucks for transportation.

One key personnel equipment item for TFR was night-vision image intensification. Night-vision devices allowed TFR and Delta to operate with deadly effect during poor lighting conditions, day or night. Aviators with AN/AVS-6 imaging systems could fly through darkness or smoke. Soldiers could use AN/PVS-7 night vision goggles to shoot, navigate, observe, or read under low-light conditions.

TFR and QRF could call on several types of helicopter. The 160th SOAR "Night Stalkers" operated 16 helicopters to support Mogadishu operations. Half of the helicopters were MH-60Ls and the rest were AH-6J and MH-6 aircraft. The MH-60L is a modified UH-60L that includes upgraded systems like forward-looking infrared (FLIR) sensors, radar, infrared jammers, night vision, and two door-mounted 7.62mm miniguns to suppress any crowds. TFR personnel could call on the AH-6 – a modified OH-6A Cayuse – for close air support. An AH-6J had two 7.62mm miniguns and two 2.75in rocket pods, each holding seven rounds. The MH-6 is an assault transport that does not carry weapons, but can carry two to three passengers internally and six on external platforms.

The 10th Mountain Division's QRF had some helicopters. They included the UH-60 for transportation, the OH-58, and the AH-1F Cobra. These helicopters formed an aviation task force. The 101st Airborne Division contributed 15 UH-60s and eight AH-1Fs. Four OH-58s came from the 10th Mountain Division and another four from Hunter Army Airfield, Savannah, Georgia. They provided scout, armed reconnaissance, and light attack capabilities, and in an emergency, these helicopters could support TFR. OH-58Ds had a mast-mounted thermal-imaging system, low-level television, and laser rangefinder and designator. The AH-1F Cobra was a more powerful attack option, and could engage tanks, armored vehicles, and buildings with TOWs.

UNOSOM II forces were problematic. US forces in Somalia had observed UN members exhibiting cautious behavior since the June 5 ambush on the Pakistanis. This "bunker mentality" was of major concern to the QRF and TFR planners. Reliance on UN forces to support major operations was in question. Several nations, if asked to support TFR, would have to request permission from their respective nations to act, since TFR was not in the direct UN chain of command. A coordinated response, therefore, might take hours.

The UNOSOM II forces came from a variety of countries and brought with them different armaments. The Indian contingent had T-72 tanks, while the Pakistani troops used donated North Atlantic Treaty Organization (NATO) M48 tanks – unfortunately, only four of the eight M48s were operational. The Malaysian soldiers drove four-wheel-drive German-made Condor armored personnel carriers (APCs). The Italians flew the A-129 Mangusta combat helicopter. The contrasting capabilities

Marines and Italian peacekeepers attempted to separate warring clans in Mogadishu. However, this only seemed to unify the rival clans against the UN efforts to bring peace to a war-torn land. One method to control Somali crowds was to barricade main streets. Clan members tore down the barricades erected by the UN throughout the city in January 1993. (DoD)

Somali warlord and militiamen

Mohamed Aideed came under great scrutiny as the architect of SNA attacks on UN personnel, especially after the June 5, 1993, attack on Pakistani peacekeepers. Keeping track of Aideed was a difficult task. UN and American officials used HUMINT and aerial surveillance to locate his whereabouts. Helicopters like the OH-58D could observe activities and report to the UN and American commands on rallies and demonstrations. Aideed and/or his key staff members would typically attend rallies to drum up support for various SNA and Habr Gidr causes. These gatherings would include efforts to demonize the UN and make claims that the United States was the enemy of Somalia and Aideed's clan. Aideed had to keep the popular support of the Somali people to survive in Mogadishu. His efforts were repaid during the October 3–4 raid, when hundreds of armed Somalis supported the SNA. Somalis are a warrior people and small arms were distributed liberally throughout Mogadishu. "Technical" vehicles provided direct fire support on a mobile platform to enhance SNA firepower.

of the UN forces created problems in command and control, logistics, and warfighting capacity.

The SNA was the opposite of TFR in many respects. Aideed's militia basically consisted of men, women, and children who used small arms. Somalia was an armed camp. Moscow had liberally supplied AK-47s to the Barre regime, while Washington had delivered M16s and other weapons, including missiles. Somali clans also had access to artillery pieces, tanks, APCs, antitank missiles, shoulder-launched SA-7 surface-to-air missiles, machine guns, and rocket-propelled grenades (RPGs), although many of the Somali heavy weapons were not operational. However, any Somali with money could purchase weapons. In the Habr Gidr-controlled Bakara Market, an Aideed stronghold in Mogadishu, the price of a RPG was $10.

The SNA could count on numbers to overwhelm any UN or TFR actions. US intelligence sources indicated the SNA had 1,000 members – the SNA itself boasted its strength at 12,000 fighters. The SNA also had a local knowledge of the area and had created an effective mobilization system that allowed Aideed's followers to mass in any controlled area in Mogadishu within 30 minutes. The SNA leadership had divided Mogadishu into 18 military sectors, each with a duty officer who could alert Aideed and others by radio. SNA fighters also played on UN and American sensibilities about "collateral damage" by using women and children as human shields and as combatants. The Somalis could hide behind these shields as counterweights to American firepower, but they also exploited women and children as spotters and observers to direct fire. The SNA and other groups could freely move within their controlled areas, and since they did not wear distinctive uniforms or insignia, UN and TFR could not positively identify them.

In many ways, Aideed's followers fought an urban guerilla war. They were using their particular strengths to fight an asymmetric conflict against the Americans. They too could concentrate firepower, by mass of numbers, yet their fighters could melt away swiftly into the streets of Mogadishu. Aideed's SNA used demonstrations and sniping to attack UN and NGO personnel, sometimes to draw peacekeepers into ambushes. Chinese- and Vietnamese-authored books on guerilla warfare inspired SNA leaders to use irregular warfare throughout their fight with the Americans and the UN. Muslim *mujahedeen* veterans, who had fought in Afghanistan, allegedly trained Somali clans on insurgent tactics and the use of RPGs and SA-7s.

The SNA leadership exploited other American weaknesses. Aideed knew that the American public would not tolerate casualties, especially in a conflict not affecting a vital national interest. Excessive casualties might force the US Congress and the public to turn against the UN and US Somali mission. Aideed's end goal was not to achieve a military victory, but to sap the will of the American public and force disengagement in Somalia.

Aideed's militia had another major advantage – they could observe TFR and UN forces. Unlike the Somalis, TFR created its sole base at the airport. Somali contract workers entered and left the airport near TFR's compound and they could report on activities to clan leadership. In addition, the airport was near some low hills from where Somalis could monitor TFR activities.

TFR RULES OF ENGAGEMENT

One of the most delicate matters faced by UNOSOM II and TFR was when to employ weapons against SNA militia or hostile crowds in an urban setting. With a global media watching, and the potential for Aideed gaining a propaganda coup if innocent civilians died, American and UN military forces had to be extremely careful when, where, and against whom to authorize deadly force. In Somalia, Garrison's men used modified UNOSOM II rules of engagement (ROE), which provided guidance for soldiers in how to act against a potential foe. UN personnel could only apply deadly force to defend themselves or persons under their protection against any real or intended hostile acts. In addition, UNOSOM II members had the authority to employ lethal means if persons attempted to resist or prevent the UN personnel from conducting their duties. Before exercising deadly force, the UN troops had to use verbal warnings. If the warnings did not work, the troops would shoot into the air to ward off any foes. If these acts did not work, then UN peacekeepers could apply deadly force if they felt threatened.

UNOSOM II leaders provided detailed guidance on a number of issues. Specifically prohibited were acts of reprisal, unnecessary collateral damage, and UN personnel using excessive force to accomplish any mission. UN forces could use "all necessary force: to disarm or demilitarize individuals and groups" if those enemies were attacking or intending harm against UNOSOM II or innocent people. In particular, UN military forces could conduct all reasonable actions to confiscate or demilitarize crew-served weapons, whether the crew appeared to be threatening or ready

to use those weapons immediately against the UN. Later, any "organized militias, technical vehicles, and other crew-served weapons" were considered immediate threats and UN personnel could engage those targets without restriction. The UN also classified as a danger any militias in vehicles appearing to advance toward UNOSOM II forces. Again, UN ground or air forces could engage these threats with deadly force.

TFR further refined the UNOSOM II ROE. Garrison's soldiers included two major situations in their ROE – one against unarmed mobs and rioters and the other concerning when to apply deadly force. Like the UN, TFR soldiers used a combination of verbal warnings and shots in the air to control and disperse a crowd. The ROE also authorized riot control agents (tear gas) and less-lethal munitions (e.g. plastic pellet grenades) to repel a hostile mob.

American SOF could use deadly force in four cases. First, Garrison authorized its use against any militiamen threatening or shooting at the TFR. Second, TFR members could shoot at any armed civilian acting with hostile intent. Third, like the UN soldiers, Garrison's military force could strike without restriction against crew-served weapons. Fourth, TFR could use lethal weapons against any unarmed but hostile crowds when verbal warnings, riot control agents, warnings shots, or less-lethal devices had failed to control the crowd.

TFR ROE also emphasized minimizing collateral casualties and property damage, and the rules called on treating any prisoners or detainees "humanely." With these rules, TFR went into combat in Mogadishu.

If helicopters left with TFR personnel, the SNA and other clans knew that they were probably on a mission. Aideed could only speculate when and where TFR would try to get him.

The SNA and the other clans had a mixed bag of weapons. Decades of Soviet and then American military aid had turned Somalia into an arms bazaar. Weapons buyers and dealers operated in the country, with arms readily available for sale in Somalia and other regions. Most heavy weapon systems, like aircraft and tanks, were in disrepair. Mortars replaced artillery for fire support, and the main weapons used by Somali clans were small arms like the AK-47 and RPG. With small arms freely available, any Mogadishu resident could fire upon TFR or UN forces throughout the city. Since there was no discernable way to tell a Habr Gidr member from an Abgal or other clan member, the SNA's ability to appear from nowhere and blend into the background was one of its greatest strengths.

TFR's Tactics and Procedures

TFR needed reliable intelligence and a rapid response to capture Aideed and his key supporters. Garrison might have only minutes to react to a report on the location or activities of one of his targets. The reaction time to launch a raid was 20–25 minutes, but TFR combat planners and operators would need to develop rapid-response tactics.

There were two likely scenarios to Aideed's capture, around which TFR designed operational templates. First, TFR personnel might have to mount an operation against a strongpoint or fortified position. Second, Aideed or one of his lieutenants might be intercepted on the ground in a vehicle. In either option, Garrison's troops could use helicopters, a ground force, or a combination of both. Combat planners believed that these tactical templates offered sufficient capability to meet their objectives. Furthermore, reliance on these templates reduced the TFR training requirements. Instead of making an extensive plan for a fleeting target, planners could direct a strike force to use either template for execution. A concern raised by some in TFR was that these scripted, limited templates might allow the Somalis to learn and adapt to these operations.

TFR developed the strongpoint position template to isolate and assault a building. Typically, four elements or "chalks" would secure street corners or areas necessary to isolate the structure. The chalks served to keep any reinforcements from attacking the building or targeted personnel from escaping. They arrived by helicopters, which inserted the soldiers by landing them on the ground or by "fast-roping," in which the soldiers used a nylon rope to deploy from a hovering helicopter. A SOF assault team would then locate the building, and while the assault team searched and seized their targets, a third platoon waited in prepositioned vehicles. Their mission was to remove or exfiltrate any prisoners and TFR personnel. The chalks left by helicopter or by the ground extraction vehicles. TFR forces also trained in inserting personnel with ground vehicles and sometimes used helicopters in diversion.

The second accepted template involved a convoy attack. Aideed and other SNA leaders traveled throughout the capital in large sports utility vehicles (SUVs). The convoy template involved tracking, stopping, and capturing personnel in these vehicles. An AH-6 would stop the vehicles by threatening

American forces could call on a helicopter force that included the OH-58 Kiowa. This scout and reconnaissance helicopter helped UN forces observe Aideed's activities throughout Mogadishu. Helicopters were a great benefit to support operations. (DoD)

US Marines, under UNITAF, conducted patrols throughout Mogadishu. This Marine is on guard for a sniper attack or sudden ambush. Fighting in an urban area frustrated peacekeepers. Determining who was a combatant or non-combatant was a constant problem that could have deadly consequences for civilians and soldiers alike. (DoD)

to fire or shooting warning rounds. Once the convoy halted, helicopters carrying TFR personnel would deploy in front and behind the target. Typically, the assault soldiers would fast-rope off a helicopter to capture the SNA leaders and all others. A blocking force, similar to the strongpoint template, landed 100–200 yards ahead of and behind the convoy.

TFR planners had the option to modify the particulars of the templates for a unique situation. Varying the templates also introduced some ambiguity in the methods used by TFR, to enhance security. The strongpoint or convoy templates could use helicopters alone, vehicles, or a combination of both. TFR did not possess any tanks or APCs – Aspin had denied earlier requests by the QFR for these vehicles. They instead had M923A2 5-ton trucks and HMMWVs, or "Humvees." The HMMWVs provided mobile fire support, since there was no American artillery assigned to Somalia.

Launching a raid required strict conditions for Garrison's approval. The start of any raid was a sighting or report of a target's location, typically from a HUMINT source. TFR officials would coordinate with Montgomery's forces before any potential mission; TFR could use the QRF and helicopters in an emergency, but TFR and the 10th Mountain Division rarely trained

A Marine mans a Mk 19 Grenade Launcher during a mission to seize illegal weapons in the Bakara Market in Mogadishu. The Bakara Market was infamous as a place where anyone could purchase or trade for automatic weapons or RPGs. Aideed's men controlled the area. (DoD)

together. Intelligence analysts verified the report using reconnaissance and other sources. To avoid any potential collateral damage, TFR officials had to confirm that no UN or NGO personnel or facilities were near the target. Once the area appeared clear, Garrison's staff coordinated and worked with UNOSOM II officials to ensure there were no conflicting issues for the mission. Garrison now had to notify CENTCOM. Once the action was approved, TFR could launch the operation.

The key to success for TFR was credible, current intelligence from various sources: UN forces; TFR's helicopters; the 10th Mountain Division's aerial resources; a detachment from the US Army's 201st Military Intelligence Brigade providing signals intelligence; national intelligence sources (like the EP-3 Reef Point aircraft); and HUMINT. However, problems did arise. Sharing HUMINT was difficult and limited. Unfortunately, a CIA handler, while drinking with some of his Somali operatives, played Russian roulette and shot himself. An intelligence agent commented, "Main source shot in the head. He's not dead yet, but we're [expletive]." The agent died while being transported out of Somalia.

TFR's Phased Operations

TFR developed a three-phased deployment into Somalia. The first phase included deployment and set-up in Mogadishu for operations. TFR personnel developed their base at the airport, and they established contacts with appropriate UN and US forces in Somalia. This phase lasted four days. TFR's second phase concentrated on trying to locate and capture Aideed. Capturing Aideed was turning into a very difficult objective. If Garrison could not get Aideed, then he would approve the last phase, which concentrated on trying to capture Aideed's top six lieutenants and neutralizing any of the SNA's critical infrastructure. If TFR was successful in taking these SNA leaders, then Aideed might need to surface to command the SNA, or surrender under pressure.

On August 28, Garrison had completed Phase I, and he and Montgomery met. The advanced command element briefed the QRF, UN, and other organizations about their mission. The 160th SOAR sought lessons learned from the 10th Mountain Division's aviation task force, and SOF aviators received orientation flights to acquaint them with the environment. TFR had taken over a large airport hanger to build living quarters, a joint operations center (JOC), intelligence fusion cell, and other facilities. Unfortunately, that night TFR received a mortar attack at 1927hrs. The newly arrived SOF units endured a 30-minute, nine-round welcome to Mogadishu. Garrison feared that if the TFR forces did not respond, then his highly trained SOF units might also develop the same "bunker mentality" as the UN troops. TFR would have to become more proactive in the search for the SNA, and start making incursions into Mogadishu. Phase II started on August 30.

TFR Operations Against Aideed and the SNA

Major General William F. Garrison initiated TFR operations soon after his

**AUGUST 30
1993**

**TFR launched
its first raid
against Aideed**

arrival in Mogadishu. His forces tested the templates, strategy, and forces in six missions before the October 3 raid. These initial raids allowed TFR to practice their skills, but also revealed that capturing Aideed was difficult. TFR had to modify its approach more toward focusing on Aideed's high-ranking lieutenants, as an indirect move against the SNA leadership.

Lig-Ligato Compound

TFR launched its first raid on August 30 in an attempt to shut down an Aideed meeting site owned by Mohamed Ibrahim Amed. Amed supported the SNA by providing information: he discussed key issues with UN officials and then relayed the details to Aideed. Aideed would attend SNA gatherings at the location within 24 hours of Amed's UN discussions. Amed's home also served as an Aideed hiding place, according to UNOSOM II intelligence sources. These sources indicated that the compound was a command-and-control center from where SNA officials had directed mortar attacks on the airport and coordinated actions against the UN and the Americans.

Early on August 30, at 0230hrs, TFR helicopter crews noticed significant vehicular and personnel activity at Amed's compound. The Americans observed that all of the compound building's lights were lit. The assault force launched at 0250hrs, using a helicopter assault with blocking forces. A ground vehicle convoy left the airport and stayed near the 21 October Triumphal Arch, also known as the K-4 Circle, to pick up any captives. This navigational landmark was a key intersection for many roads, including a route to the American embassy compound and into downtown Mogadishu.

The assault force would search two buildings. Once in position, the Delta members hit the first building at 0309hrs and secured it by 0316hrs. The second building was cleared at 0321hrs. Delta commandos did not find Aideed, but they did take nine captives, some documents, a radio, a quantity of *khat*, large amounts of currency, and weapons. After further investigation, TFR realized the buildings were former UN facilities and that their captives were UN Development Program employees who had failed to move out of the buildings after being told to do so by UNOSOM personnel. American officials released them to UN control. The raid was a major embarrassment.

The 160th SOAR operated specially modified MH-60 Black Hawk helicopters. These aircraft could operate in all weathers and at night to support SOF worldwide. Sensors and other capabilities allowed pilots to conduct actions throughout Mogadishu. (DoD)

Old Russian Compound

The next mission was an attempt to capture Aideed near the former Russian embassy in Mogadishu. TFR helicopters left the airport at 0227hrs on September 7. Delta captured 17 USC/SNA militiamen, including the SNA paymaster, but the assault force failed to arrest Aideed. The ground vehicle reaction force took small-arms and RPG fire from locations near the parade-reviewing stand on Via Lenin and the Digfer Hospital. TFR responded with .50cal machine-gun and Mk 19 grenade support from HMMWVs. MH-60 and AH-6 miniguns supported the vehicles.

Jialiou House

This raid focused on trying to arrest Aideed again. Rangers escorting TFR's J-2 director saw Aideed leaving the Italian embassy on September 14. The J-2 director had departed the airport in a three-vehicle convoy to address some issues with his counterpart in the Italian embassy. One of those issues regarded alleged coordination between Aideed and the Italians. Rangers saw an individual who looked like Aideed leaving the embassy at 1142hrs in a Toyota Land Cruiser. Helicopters tracked the vehicle as it made two stops. A person left the vehicle at the first stop, but J-2 analysts believed that the most likely location of Aideed was at the second stop.

An assault force left at 1239hrs from the airport and an assault on the second stop location was conducted at 1245hrs. The ground convoy passed near the first stop, where they saw individuals with weapons, but they did not enter it. The assault force did capture 39 people and a cache of weapons, documents, and radios. TFR evacuated the detainees to the airport and then to a Pakistani detention center. Unfortunately, the intelligence sources identified the captives as members of a rival clan of Aideed's. The person believed to have been Aideed was former Somali police chief General Ahmed Jialiou, a UN ally. TFR released Jialiou to the UN.

Radio Aideed

One means Aideed used to send propaganda and messages throughout Mogadishu was through a low-power radio transmitter, Radio Aideed. The site was south of the Bakara Market. Although transmitting for only three hours per evening, it served as an Aideed command-and-control mechanism, and hence was a major target for TFR officials to shut down. TFR arrived in ground vehicles supported by two Black Hawks to the area on September 17. At 0254hrs, TFR started to search five buildings for the radio transmitter, but did not find it. The SOF did kill a SNA militia junior officer who had participated in the June 5 ambush on the Pakistani UN forces. Later information sources confirmed that TFR was close to the radio transmitter and had missed it by 30 yards.

Osman Atto's Garage

TFR targeted Osman Atto, Aideed's chief advisor and financier. Atto's repair garage served as a source of SNA income and as a meeting site. TFR initiated the operation at 0826hrs on September 18, with helicopters monitoring the garage. Observers witnessed Atto and others near the garage, and once TFR's J-2 confirmed Atto's presence, a helicopter assault force and blocking party arrived around 0847hrs. A ground convoy left the airport to assist the assault force. The raid netted eight detainees, but Atto was not among them. The Americans took RPG and small-arms fire from the parade-reviewing stand and the Digfer Hospital, in a similar way to the raid on the Old Russian Compound. TFR evacuated the detainees by helicopter, and the assault force left by ground vehicles.

American forces in Somalia did not have any APCs. Although the presence of such vehicles would not have prevented the downing of the two MH-60Ls, they could have protected the rescue attempts. These M2 Bradley APCs are going to Somalia after the October 3–4 raid. (DoD)

Capturing Osman Atto

TFR tried to get Atto again on September 21. Intelligence sources reported Atto in a light blue vehicle headed west on Armed Forces Road at 0910hrs, and helicopters tracked the vehicle as it headed toward the Digfer Hospital. TFR helicopters, with Delta and Rangers, positioned themselves near Atto's vehicle at 0941hrs and they executed the convoy assault template. The passengers and Atto scattered. TFR soldiers watched them run into a compound consisting of four buildings, so Garrison's men changed the template to a strongpoint assault. Delta members captured Atto in the second building searched, along with three males, in the building's kitchen. TFR secured the entire compound at 1001hrs and identified Atto at 1028hrs. Garrison turned Atto and the other detainees over to UNOSOM II officials. TFR soldiers counted 12 RPG rounds fired at helicopters. Somali gunfire most likely caused minor tail rotor damage to a MH-60L.

Atto's capture provided a welcomed boost in morale to TFR. Unfortunately, it drove Aideed and his other senior officials to go further underground and complicated TFR's ability to gather information on Aideed.

The American embassy in Mogadishu had suffered considerable damage when Washington abandoned it during the Somali civil war against Barre. The embassy was a convenient target for Aideed to attack. The headquarters for the QRF is shown next to the embassy's grounds. (DoD)

PLAN

TFR had now attempted several raids to capture Aideed, catch his most important aides, and degrade key SNA infrastructure. The SNA leadership were aware of TFR's primary objective – get Aideed. Still, the Americans had one major advantage over the SNA, mobility by helicopter. TFR exploited their use of helicopters to concentrate military forces at will, night or day. Although the helicopters seemed impregnable by virtue of their speed and armament, they could also become a major problem if the aircraft themselves became targets. One enemy means to this end was to use RPGs to bring down a helicopter. TFR and QRF commanders noticed the SNA militia's increased use of this weapon.

Aideed experimented with ways to attract and destroy American helicopters. One scheme was to conduct mortar attacks to hit UN and other targets. The Somalis had conducted four continuous nights of 60mm and 120mm mortar fire in September, while the QRF tried to attack them via air and ground forces. Somali fire harassed Americans, but it also served to lure helicopters to an area where the SNA could engage them with ground fire and RPGs.

UH-60 Black Hawks gave 10th Mountain Division soldiers the ability to move quickly throughout Mogadishu and areas nearby. Unfortunately, SNA RPG gunners shot down one of the Black Hawks on September 25, 1993, a week before the battle of Mogadishu. (DoD)

Aideed supporters experimented with fuse-modified RPGs, and shot down a UH-60 Black Hawk at 0200hrs on September 25. The crew had investigated SNA activities near Mogadishu's main seaport, the New Port. The helicopter was flying about 150 knots at an altitude of only 100ft. The RPG exploded in the cabin and killed three crew members. The 160th SOAR pilots believed it was a lucky shot, and that their training and experienced operators allowed them to fly fast and with irregular flight patterns that would evade RPGs. In contrast, the pilots supporting the QRF flew too low and slow. The UH-60 destruction was a huge SNA psychological victory – the Somalis demonstrated that they could best the Americans.

If the SNA could knock out Black Hawks, then they could isolate the Americans. To avert casualties, the Americans would probably mount extraordinary efforts to rescue their colleagues. Aideed also believed that his Somalis, unlike the Americans, were willing to die fighting. His massed forces might catch the TFR or the QRF in a massive ambush that would result in a strategic victory, namely the withdrawal of the UN and America from Somalia.

TFR and the QRF Prepare for Action

TFR waited for another chance to strike. It still required the few HUMINT contacts in Mogadishu or aerial reconnaissance to make a positive identification of the SNA leadership. Garrison did have the advantage of time. Aideed and his leadership would eventually surface to take charge of the Habr Gidr, or else rival clans might move into their territory.

On Sunday morning, October 3, UN and American personnel were not engaged in any major operations. However, a CISE counterintelligence team had scheduled a meeting with some clan elders at the New Port to gather any information about the SNA intentions and Aideed's whereabouts. At 1030hrs, a command-detonated mine wounded three Marines and killed the CISE team's Somali interpreter in a HMMWV. The day had not started well.

Most Sundays brought out SNA rallies, in which speakers denounced the UN and America. Omar Salad, a key Aideed political adviser, spoke to a crowd at a parade-reviewing stand on the Via Lenin near the Coca-Cola bottling plant. Salad was one of the six SNA lieutenants identified for capture. As he left the rally, aerial reconnaissance assets tracked his movement in a white Toyota Land Cruiser to the Bakara Market area, deep in Aideed-controlled territory. Many Americans called these vehicles "Klingon Cruisers," after the Star Trek series. Garrison had heard CENTCOM warnings not to enter the area unless there was no other way to get Aideed or the SNA leadership. The TFR commander commented, "If we go into the vicinity of the Bakara Market, there's no question we'll win the gunfight. But we might lose the war."

HUMINT sources indicated that Salad was meeting Colonel Abdi Hassan Awale, Aideed's Minister of the Interior, in the area. Aideed was soon to announce that Awale was going to become his Foreign Minister. This location was in a house about a block from the Olympic Hotel close to National Street, a major east–west road. The Olympic Hotel was a known gathering place for SNA leadership meetings. At 1350hrs, the TFR

SEPTEMBER 25 1993

QRF Black Hawk shot down near Mogadishu

intelligence fusion cell analysts received the report. They also had indications that Aideed was going to be present at this gathering. By 1403hrs, three helicopters – one OH-58 Kiowa and two Little Birds – launched to observe the area near the Olympic Hotel. If TFR could capture all three, the SNA would collapse and the main obstacle to the UN would now be defeated.

TFR personnel followed the approved raid notification protocol. The information about the meeting appeared valid when confirmed by HUMINT. The JOC alerted the American liaison officer at UNOSOM II headquarters. Other TFR officers notified UNOSOM II officials about the mission and ensured that no NGO or UN activities were in the area. Garrison informed Montgomery of the possible mission's location and targets. When told of the location in the Bakara Market, Montgomery said "That's really Indian country. That's a bad place." Additionally, the TFR staff contacted other government agencies of the mission too. By 1505hrs, Garrison's staff told the QRF and 10th Mountain Division's aviation units of an impending raid. This allowed the TFR to confirm there were no other aircraft flying in the area. The notification also put the QRF on a heightened alert. All seemed ready for action, with ground forces primed and airspace cleared for helicopter deployments from the airport. TFR elements would now prepare to move from their base to the Bakara Market area. Observers flying in OH-58s, Little Birds, and an EP-3E watched vehicular traffic. The EP-3 transmitted television images to Garrison at the JOC. The soldiers would have to move quickly to the site, surprise any SNA security, capture the targets, and leave immediately.

Heavy weapons, like artillery and tanks, were scattered throughout Somalia. Typically these weapons were not operational due to neglect. Still, artillery pieces like this one could inflict severe damage on UN operations if clan members could operate them. (DoD)

OCTOBER 3 1993

1350hrs TFR analysts receive intelligence of Aideed's location

The TFR intelligence fusion cell also relied on HUMINT. A Somali agent, from the Abgal clan, was going to identify the target building via a marked car. American airborne assets watched him. The agent successfully signaled the location of the target house by raising the hood of his car.

The major ground contingency was the QRF. This force came from elements of the 2nd Battalion, 14th Infantry Regiment. The QRF mission rotated among three companies, and the companies switched activities every three days. One company performed security and training activities while the other two provided protection of main supply routes throughout Mogadishu or acted as the QRF. While acting as the QRF, the company pulling that duty could call on the battalion headquarters and transportation personnel to augment the combat capability. This force included battalion engineers, scouts, psychological operations team, medical personnel, and fire-support observers. QRF's official reaction time was 30 minutes, but the company could get ready in about half that time. In an emergency, the other two companies could complement the QRF – they could be ready in about an hour. Soldiers in the QRF had heavy trucks and HMMWVs, or could use UH-60s from an assault helicopter battalion. They also had the services of an attack helicopter battalion for close air support.

Black Hawks and Little Birds

TFR planners recommended using the strongpoint template against the target, a three-story building holding unknown numbers of SNA followers. The house was on a block near a north–south byway, the Hawlwadig Road. The plan was rather simple and TFR members had conducted it many times.

Rangers, using four MH-60L Black Hawks, would form the four chalks. Teams of Delta, using four MH-6 Little Birds, each helicopter carrying four soldiers on external boards, would secure the building, search, and capture the SNA targets. MH-60Ls would carry more Delta and other SOF members near the building. A C2 (command-and-control) Black Hawk helicopter supported the raid, and it contained the assault commander, the air mission commander, and the fire-support officer. These individuals had a bird's-eye view to observe and direct actions above the mission.

The assault force could also call on AH-6Js, machine-gun and rocket-armed versions of the MH-6s, which could provide close air support to forces on the ground. Two AH-6Js would pass over the targeted building first before the MH-6s landed. The last major aerial resource was a single combat search-and-rescue (CSAR) MH-60L that hovered at 80ft, waiting for the airborne C2 helicopter to call it into action. If the Somalis did shoot down a helicopter, then the CSAR force – three USAF special tactics airmen, five Delta, and seven Rangers – would fast-rope to the crash site to secure it and then recover any personnel. It served as the only immediate contingency force. After the MH-60Ls dropped off their Rangers to create the chalks, they stayed aloft to support the mission. Other MH-60Ls had Delta snipers to provide added precise firepower and were available to conduct medical evacuations. Nine Black Hawks would fly into Mogadishu. Typically, the MH-60Ls flew at about 500ft. Curiously, this altitude was set below the RPG burnout time.

The worst scenario for TFR involved a helicopter shoot-down in the Bakara Market. Getting to a downed crew would be difficult, especially if the SNA massed at the crash site. TFR, QRF, and UN forces might require time to find, secure, and extract the crew. Unfortunately, the crew might die or become prisoners in the meantime.

The plan also included a ground convoy or ground reaction force to pick up any SNA detainees and extract the TFR. Lieutenant Colonel Danny McKnight, the Ranger battalion commander, took charge of nine HMMWVs and three M923A2 5-ton trucks to pick up the prisoners and TFR personnel. Unfortunately, TFR did not have M1A1 Abrams tanks or M2 Bradley fighting vehicles. Montgomery had failed to receive permission from Washington to get these vehicles due to force structure restrictions. The HMMWVs did have an assortment of weapons to protect a convoy, but the 5-ton trucks were unarmored – soldiers had to place sandbags around each vehicle to add to their protection.

The ground convoy would leave the airport compound when the helicopters left to raid the target building. McKnight had to stay a few blocks away to await a prearranged signal to drive north past the Olympic Hotel and stop to pick up the "precious cargo" and raiding force. They then would all leave.

Somali Preparations

Although the SNA did not have the formal training of SOF personnel, they were fiercely loyal to the clan and to Aideed. Many were not afraid of dying

Many American military leaders wanted armor for UNOSOM II. When UNITAF left, American tanks, like this M1A1 Abrams, departed too. Armor under American control could have speeded up rescue efforts during *Gothic Serpent* by breaking through Somali blockades and providing direct fire support. (DoD)

US SOF IN SOMALIA

The use of TFR was not the first instance of US SOF activities in Somalia. Army, Navy, and Air Force SOF units participated from the beginning of Washington's initial famine relief efforts to the end of American commitments supporting UN operations. Detachments from the Army's 2nd Battalion, 5th Special Forces Group (Airborne) supported initial food shipments under Operation *Provide Relief*, starting on August 15, 1992. These detachments provided security to the USAF missions, but also accomplished other activities, such as assessing the local conditions and threats throughout southern Somalia, reconnaissance near airfields, and gathering information for future ground missions. Also, while other USAF aircraft delivered relief supplies to famine-touched areas, a C-130 circled the airfield with two SOF vehicles. This force acted as an airborne security element to respond to an emergency at the airport during aid unloading and distribution.

Under Operation *Restore Hope*, US Marines operating under UNITAF landed near Mogadishu. A Navy SEAL platoon and Special Boat Unit provided an invaluable service by gathering information about potential landing sites along the coast. American officials wanted to land Marine Corps units quietly to secure port facilities and intimidate the Somali clans. At night, 12 Navy SEALs reconnoitered the beaches to get hydrographic information on depths, beach conditions, presence of obstacles, and other information to guide an amphibious landing. This information allowed the USS *Tripoli*, *Juneau*, and *Rushmore* to deploy the Marine Expeditionary Unit (MEU) on the beaches on December 7, 1992. Unfortunately, the media got wind of the landing. There was some concern in Washington that Somali agitators might contest the American deployment going into Mogadishu. Instead, the reporters recorded the night landing under glaring camera lights, but the action occurred without major incident.

The SEALs also supported other UN operations. They conducted a survey of the port in Kismayo under fire, and also executed reconnaissance missions against gun smugglers. These missions resulted in further military operations against those smugglers. SEALs supported a security mission to protect President George H.W. Bush, when he visited Somalia before his presidential term expired. Indian commandos also received special training for their Somali deployment.

SOF operations expanded on January 12, 1993, with the creation of the JSOFOR. Elements of JSOFOR made initial contact with local leaders and clans, gathered information on areas for future relief operations, and assessed potential areas for force protection and security missions. Civil affairs personnel coordinated humanitarian relief, medical, and engineering civic action programs for the Somalis.

Washington also deployed a Joint Psychological Operations Task Force. Psychological operations included printing and distributing a newspaper (the *Rajo* or "The Truth"), newsletters, and leaflets. The unit could also provide a mobile loudspeaker system to transmit pre-recorded or speaker programs to the Somalis. Linguists and interpreters went on missions with Marine Corps and Army field units to communicate with local residents. The task force also created a radio program to broadcast a 45-minute, twice-a-day program with news, music, entertainment, and other information to counter Aideed's radio broadcasts.

The Air Force Special Operations Command (AFSOC) sent four AC-130H Spectre gunships to Somalia after the June 5 attack on Pakistani UN soldiers. These aircraft operated out of Mombasa, Kenya, a location that avoided stationing additional Americans in Somalia. General Hoar had requested the AC-130s through the Joint Staff to strike Aideed's militia and their infrastructure. During their deployment, the aircrews flew 32 missions from June 7 to July 14, and conducted eight combat sorties from June 11 to 17. The AC-130s destroyed weapons storage facilities, vehicle concentrations, a "Radio Mogadishu" station (another one of Aideed's propaganda arms), an armored vehicle compound, and a munitions factory. Using their heavy firepower, the AC-130s created fear among Somalis because of their destructive power, day or night. They had special sensors that allowed them to provide detection and tracking information to give ground commanders precision fire.

After the October 3 raid in Mogadishu, Washington sent additional Army and Marine units to Somalia to stabilize the situation. Still, President Bill Clinton ordered the American deployment to end by March 1994. AFSOC redeployed two AC-130Hs into Kenya. Navy SEAL Teams 2 and 8 provided security, sniper, reconnaissance, and surveillance activities. Although most American military units left Somalia in March 1994, the SEALs supported the UN until their withdrawal from Somalia on March 3, 1995.

for their cause, and their leaders believed mass of fire and sheer numbers would overcome the Americans in certain conditions. The best situation for the SNA was to isolate the Americans and overwhelm them.

The chief SNA commander in Mogadishu was Colonel Sharif Hassan Giumale. Giumale was a former Somali Army brigade commander. He had attended a Soviet military academy in Odessa for three years and completed further training in Italy. Living near the Olympic Hotel, Giumale served as the Deputy Commander SNA High Commission on Defense. His experience included combat against Ethiopian forces under the Barre administration. He would be in a perfect location to direct operations against the TFR.

Giumale observed the TFR tactics and believed that the SNA militia's advantages of local knowledge, mass, persistence, and willingness to fight would overcome the Americans. He also thought the Americans suffered from overconfidence. Giumale was especially surprised at the continued American use of template operations. One of Giumale's commanders, Colonel Ali Aden, commented, "If you use one tactic twice, you should not use it a third time and the Americans already had done basically the same thing six times." Garrison and TFR planners had tried to hide the templates by varying infiltration or extraction by truck, helicopter, or a combination. Additionally, 160th SOAR aviators flew training missions at all hours of the day and conducted diversionary sorties to confuse the Somalis. Unfortunately, the lack of time to react to a mission, the exposure of the airport, and limited forces forced Garrison to use the templates repeatedly. One advantage the Americans used was operating at night, which could mask any template use, but the mission's timing forced TFR to work in daylight.

The SNA militia would have to react quickly to any incursion into their controlled area. Giumale and Aideed's leadership created a structure of 18 military sectors around Mogadishu. Although the American forces tried to jam radios (like Radio Aideed) and cell phones throughout the city to disrupt SNA command and control, the militia still had an effective communications capability in the form of runners.

Aideed relied on a Somali public that had turned against the UN and the Americans. US combat activities, Somali casualties, and the continued occupation had pushed the Somali public opinion against UNOSOM II. UN action did not seem like peacekeeping and appeared, to some Somalis, to have lost its impartiality by attacking Aideed. The July 12 helicopter attack and continued fighting around Mogadishu had hardened public anger against the Americans. Irregular forces who did not have formal military training were willing to help the SNA, whether it was through reporting on the TFR activities, sniping, or spotting for SNA fighters. These groups also provided people to surround the Americans to slow down any ground movement, intimidate defenders, and construct blockades. Once the Americans were on the streets and isolated, Giumale could delay any reinforcements' arrival by building obstructions topped with burning rubber tires and debris.

THE RAID

The events of the October 3–4 raid in Mogadishu had profound consequences for Somalia, the UN, the United States, and Operation *Gothic Serpent*. The raid was initially planned as a simple "grab and snatch" mission to get two key Aideed lieutenants. Unfortunately, for TFR, the mission transformed into a major firefight that dragged on for about 14 hours and had tremendous impact on the American public's mind. Indeed, the battle of Mogadishu and its aftermath affected Washington's foreign policy for years, especially in Africa.

The start of the seventh raid for TFR began with a Somali HUMINT agent identifying a building where Salad and Awale wanted to conduct a

This AC-130H target photograph illustrates the Olympic Hotel, near the meeting house with Salad and Awale. The Olympic Hotel was a known hangout for Aideed and the SNA leadership. It bordered the Bakara Market. (Col Mike Marra)

meeting. TFR planners received all necessary coordination to launch the raid, and by 1415hrs, TFR officials had made the area around the targeted building off limits to all UN activities. Montgomery, UN officials, the QRF, American aviation sources, and others knew that the Rangers and Delta (also called the "D-boys") were going into the area for an operation. At most, the mission might last 35–40 minutes from start to finish. The Rangers and Delta had performed similar missions in the past, but although he used veteran forces, Garrison had some concerns. He had believed that if the mission lasted more than 30 minutes in the Bakara Market, then Aideed's supporters would engage TFR in a prolonged brawl.

"Irene": Going into the "Black Sea"

At 1523hrs, TFR received approval to begin the operation. The Rangers started moving. Two platoons of Company B, 3rd Battalion, 75th Ranger Regiment, commanded by Captain Mike Steele, would load into four MH-60Ls to form the blocking chalks. The third platoon, with McKnight, operated the ground convoy to exfiltrate the prisoners and potentially all of the Rangers and Delta. Delta and other SOF started to get into the MH-6s and other MH-60s. TFR elements had much practice in quickly readying for a helicopter-borne assault and all were loaded for their mission by 1529hrs. For the first time during the Somali deployment, Garrison ordered the AH-6s to carry 2.75in rocket pods, an ominous sign of expected resistance. TFR pilots would enter the Bakara Market into an area called the "Black Sea" – a warren of shanties and buildings occupied by Aideed supporters, who would kill any UN or American soldier for an SNA reward. From the air, Mogadishu looked like a patchwork of nondescript shacks with a confusing array of alleys and roads.

During the raid's preparations, the Rangers determined what equipment and supplies to carry. Many Rangers believed that they would return before

This training shot illustrates how Delta members would land near their target. The Delta soldiers would then secure and search the target house and prepare the prisoners for transport back to the Mogadishu International Airport and further processing. (DoD)

OCTOBER 3
1993

1523hrs
TFR authorized to
carry out raid

THE BATTLE OF MOGADISHU

OCTOBER 3–4, 1993

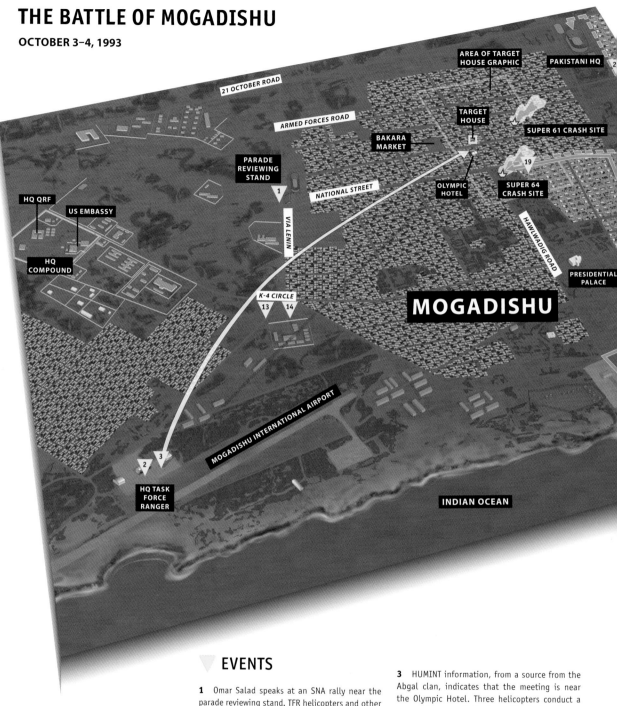

21 OCTOBER ROAD

ARMED FORCES ROAD

AREA OF TARGET
HOUSE GRAPHIC

PAKISTANI HQ

TARGET
HOUSE

SUPER 61 CRASH SITE

BAKARA
MARKET

PARADE
REVIEWING
STAND

NATIONAL STREET

OLYMPIC
HOTEL

SUPER 64
CRASH SITE

HQ QRF

US EMBASSY

VIA LENIN

HAWLWADIG ROAD

HQ
COMPOUND

PRESIDENTIAL
PALACE

K-4 CIRCLE

MOGADISHU

MOGADISHU INTERNATIONAL AIRPORT

HQ TASK
FORCE
RANGER

INDIAN OCEAN

▼ EVENTS

1 Omar Salad speaks at an SNA rally near the parade reviewing stand. TFR helicopters and other aerial assets monitor Salad's movements back to the Bakara Market area.

2 At 1350hrs the TFR JOC begins planning a raid to capture Salad and Abdi Awale near the Olympic Hotel after reports of a possible meeting. Garrison's staff coordinates with UNOSOM and Montgomery. Garrison receives permission from CENTCOM to execute mission.

3 HUMINT information, from a source from the Abgal clan, indicates that the meeting is near the Olympic Hotel. Three helicopters conduct a reconnaissance mission to verify the location at 1459hrs. The meeting house is about two blocks north of the hotel.

4 After the JOC verified the location, TFR coordinated with UN and Montgomery, assault force loaded, and helicopters readied, Garrison launches the helicopters from Mogadishu airport at 1532hrs. The distance from the airport to target house is three miles.

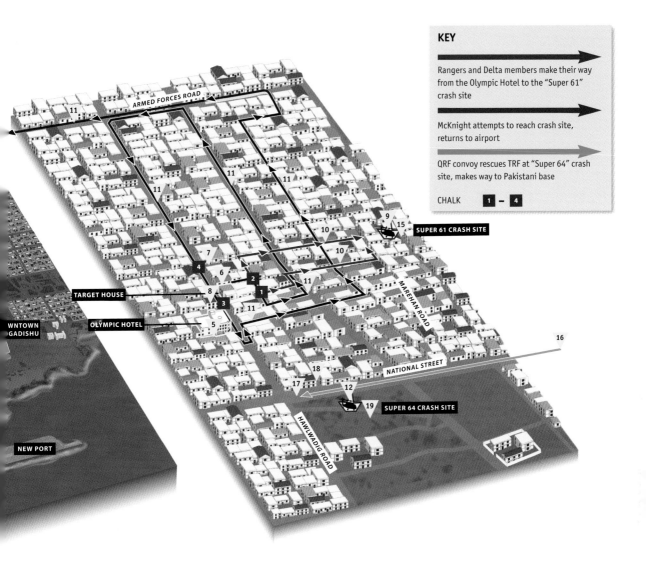

5 TFR ground convoy (ground reaction force), composed of nine HMMWVs and three M923A2 5-ton trucks, leaves the airport at 1535hrs and arrives ten minutes later near the Olympic Hotel.

6 TFR assault helicopters sweep the target building at 1540hrs. Delta members land and search the building at 1542hrs.

7 Chalks set up around target area. One Ranger is injured fast-roping at Chalk 1.

8 Around 1600hrs, the ground convoy starts to pick up prisoners. Chalks start moving towards the trucks and HMMWVs. Three HMMWVs depart main convoy with the injured Ranger to the airport.

9 At 1620hrs, Super 61 hit by RPG and crashes. Super 68 hit by RPG, forced to return to the airport at 1628hrs. An MH-6 lands and evacuates two wounded at 1631hrs.

10 Rangers and Delta members from the assault force move to Super 61's crash site. McKnight told to move, with remaining vehicles, prisoners, and personnel to crash site.

11 McKnight's convoy fails to reach crash site, circles area. McKnight returns to the airport due to casualties.

12 Super 64 downed by RPG at 1641hrs. Gordon and Shugart drop from Super 62 to assist. Super 62 hit by a RPG, goes to the New Port.

13 A contingent of Rangers, trying to reach the second crash site, link up with McKnight at the K-4 Circle. The combined convoy leaves at 1740hrs. The Ranger contingent cannot break through Somali blockades, returns with McKnight.

14 QRF attempts to reach Super 64. The 10th Mountain Division QRF company gets involved in firefight at the K-4 Circle at 1745hrs. They return to the airport.

15 Super 66 resupplies TFR at the Super 61 crash site at approximately 1910hrs.

16 The QRF arrives at the New Port at 2200hrs and leaves at 2323hrs with the Malaysians and Pakistanis.

17 Two Condors turn down the wrong street near Super 64.

18 QRF elements dismount and move towards Super 61 at about 0036hrs. They link up with TFR at 0155hrs.

19 Americans secure Super 64's crash site at 0227hrs. There are no signs of survivors. Black Hawk destroyed at 0300hrs. Missing QRF members from the two errant Condors reach American lines. They evacuate to the Pakistani base.

20 TFR moves out of Super 61 crash site starting at 0542hrs. There is not enough transport capability, some Rangers forced to move on foot. Rescue force returns to Pakistani base near the stadium at 0630hrs.

The K-4 Circle was a site of several key activities during the October 3-4 raid. The site was near a parade-reviewing stand where Salad attended a rally on Sunday morning. SNA supporters also fought against US rescue convoys passing near the K-4 Circle. (DoD)

dark. Since the Rangers would operate in full daylight and return before sunset, none of them packed night-vision goggles. Others did not bother to carry any water or rations. Rangers also carried the minimum load of ammunition. Other equipment stayed behind. Because of the heat, anticipated short duration of the mission, and small chance of a firefight, soldiers took out plates from their body armor.

Not all of the 3rd Battalion soldiers went on the raid. Part of battalion needed to remain at the airport to secure the base and perform other functions. Since the deployment was kept at a minimal manpower level, relatively few troops went on the mission. There was a small reserve for any immediate contingency other than the use of the CSAR helicopter hovering nearby, the ground convoy for the return trip, and the one light infantry company from the QRF. The UNOSOM II forces could help, but it was problematic since organizing and coordinating the UN to move would take time and required those units getting appropriate approvals from their national authorities for their use.

Once ready for action, Garrison authorized release of the codename "Irene" and the seventh TFR mission began. The MH-60, MH-6, and AH-6 aerial force left at 1532hrs. The helicopters only had to cross three miles of ground to reach the target building, two or three minutes' flying time. Crews would approach the target area from the north and strike south.

Meanwhile, at 1535hrs, McKnight and the 12-vehicle convoy left the airport to position themselves south of the target, so that they would be close enough to recover the assault and chalk forces quickly. Somali observers could see all of the preparations and movements going on within the airport. The only question for these onlookers was whether the TFR action was one of the numerous training exercises or a real mission to capture Aideed. McKnight then ordered the convoy on to a road heading northeast to the 21 October Triumphal Arch. McKnight moved north on the Via Lenin near the parade-reviewing stand where Salad had spoken to SNA supporters that morning. The HMMWVs and trucks proceeded to National Street and then toward the Olympic Hotel. There were no major incidents on the trip and McKnight got into the area.

Orbiting OH-58D and EP-3E aircraft acted as the "eyes" for the ground convoy to guide them through Mogadishu's spider's web of roads, streets, alleys, and obstacles. Unfortunately, the EP-3 crew could not directly communicate with the ground convoy because of procedural rules. The Navy EP-3 crew would therefore have to transmit their information through the TFR JOC for Garrison's staff to review then communicate directions. EP-3 cameras transmitted live television feeds that provided Garrison and JOC controllers a way to view the activities as the mission unfolded. McKnight's ground convoy was only one of several elements in the raid, and Garrison had to make decisions based on the impact of the entire mission, not just on the convoy. JOC staff then passed the information to the C2 MH-60 for transmission to McKnight with instructions. This process dragged out the time it took to warn the convoy about an obstacle or ambush, as the vehicles sped through a city filled with people, civilian vehicles, animals, and other obstructions to traffic. Furthermore, as the vehicles drove around the city, if troops received a delayed warning then the drivers could miss an exit or turn on to a wrong road. This problem would magnify issues for TFR under combat conditions, with smoke from burning tires or other impediments.

The airborne reconnaissance force did notice two roadblocks with burning tires during the trip to the target area and had warned McKnight. Soon, the Somalis would create more blockades manned by angry, armed SNA supporters. McKnight led the convoy to an area about 200 yards south of the target building and waited for the call to exit the area. His convoy parked close to the Olympic Hotel at 1545hrs. TFR planners thought 160 personnel, 12 ground vehicles, and 19 helicopters and aircraft for the mission was sufficient. Everything seemed ready to execute. Hopefully, the two lieutenants and the SNA members in the building would cooperate and not resist, but simply surrender.

Leading off the mission were the MH-6s with the assault force. Captain Scott Miller commanded the Delta unit, and AH-6s accompanied the MH-6s for close air support. Next in formation were the MH-60s. Rangers from the 1st and 2nd Platoons of B Company, commanded by First Lieutenants Thomas Di Tomasso and Larry Perino, would make up the chalks. The 1st Platoon had responsibility for Chalks 1 and 3 and 2nd Platoon Chalks 2 and 4. Each chalk would have between 12 and 15 soldiers, led by an officer or non-commissioned officer (NCO). A single helicopter would deploy all of the Rangers for a single chalk. Steele accompanied his men on the mission – he would also be in charge of securing the outside perimeter for a block in each direction. The Delta teams had responsibility for the target building alone. The mission had two commanders controlling the assault and the blocking forces, so no single mission commander was on the ground for TFR.

Rangers would fast-rope into their chalk positions after the MH-6s dropped the Delta members on ground near the building, where they would

OCTOBER 3 1993

1532hrs Helicopter elements take off on raid

PREVIOUS PAGES
The primary objective for TFR was to capture two major SNA figures, Awale and Salad, at a three-story meeting house near the Olympic Hotel. The raid went smoothly, but SNA supporters and Mogadishu residents continued to attack the Ranger chalks and Delta commandos around the target. Rangers drove the ground convoy vehicles to remove the 24 detainees. While loading the SNA operatives, TFR soldiers continued to be attacked and the Somalis destroyed one 5-ton truck. The Americans returned fire against their foes. Snipers and minigunners on MH-60Ls provided some fire suppression, but could not halt the Somali onslaught. Despite the heavy weapons on the HMMWVs and the helicopters, the TFR moved fast to get out. Part of the convoy had to return immediately with an injured Ranger, after he fell while fast-roping from a helicopter. Unfortunately, after loading the prisoners, the convoy tried and failed to access the Super 61 crash site. Several Americans and Somalis in the convoy became casualties during the attempts to reach Super 61.

take control of the structure and any persons inside. As Delta teams entered the building, others would seal it from the outside and keep any SNA members from escaping. The assault landing and chalk set-up would take only a few minutes to accomplish, if all went well.

This choreographed mission faced some obstacles. Power lines, telephone wires, disabled vehicles, debris, and dust "brownouts" often became hazards during helicopter assaults. The Rangers had to fast-rope about 45ft from the helicopters instead of trying to land, because of the obstructions on the ground. While fast-roping down from a helicopter, Rangers could be enveloped by heavy dust and lose their vision and orientation. The brownout conditions could also interfere with soldiers' ability to locate individuals shooting at the chalk. Typically, after establishing a perimeter, the Rangers would clear an area for a landing zone to allow the MH-60s to pick them up after the mission. Unfortunately, the large amounts of ground litter and growing crowds made this impossible. A hostile, armed crowd could easily damage a helicopter on the ground. All of the TFR and Somali prisoners would have to return to the base via McKnight's ground convoy.

At about 1540hrs, an AH-6 swept the top of the target building to ensure no opposition was present that could interfere with the raid. Two AH-6s – Barbers 51 and 52 – circled about 300ft above the target building, in case the Delta or Rangers needed fire support from their rockets or 7.62mm miniguns. Four MH-6s then landed near the target. The assault began about 1542hrs – the Delta forces started to secure the building, and more Delta reinforcements arrived. An MH-60L – Super 61 – piloted by Chief Warrant Officer Cliff Wolcott, delivered additional Delta commandos to support the initial strike. It took only 45 seconds for Wolcott's passengers to exit the helicopter. Then Super 61, like other MH-60Ls, remained in the area to serve as a means to extract any TFR member, fire its two miniguns to keep a crowd at bay, or shoot any gunmen, especially ones carrying RPGs. Not all of Wolcott's passengers had left Super 61, however – Delta snipers remained onboard to pick off SNA militia or other targets.

The chalks had started to form. The Rangers dropped out of their helicopters to create blocking positions at four corners of the area around the target. Rangers in each chalk planned to form an "L" perimeter at each assigned corner. The raid was proceeding as planned until there was an accident. As the Rangers in Chalk 4 left the helicopter, a new soldier to TFR, Private First Class Todd Blackburn, fell 40ft on to the ground while trying to fast-rope into position. Staff Sergeant Matt Eversmann, the chalk leader, requested a medical evacuation for his unconscious soldier. He was bleeding from the nose, ear, and mouth. Medics stabilized his condition, but the Rangers could not clear a landing zone and let any MH-60 or MH-6 take him out – he would have to wait for McKnight's ground convoy. Blackburn was the first of several casualties that TFR would suffer.

Ominously, the commotion from the Black Hawks and Little Birds had stirred the local population. Eversmann and others were now taking heavy fire from all directions. Once the Delta and Rangers began to appear, the Black Sea residents alerted SNA officials of the raid. Aideed's followers began to mobilize and arm themselves. Giumale, the SNA militia commander in Mogadishu, started to orchestrate a response to the TFR incursion into his territory. One of his main objectives was to isolate any Americans. Actions like blockading areas, setting up traps, and shooting down helicopters would all help with this goal. By radio, Giumale notified sector commanders to move SNA militia to meet the Americans. Militiamen organized ambushes along routes most likely to be taken by vehicles from Mogadishu airport or the American 10th Mountain Division compound. Other militiamen, along with city residents, reacted to the gunfire and ran toward the target building. Militia from all points of the compass drove with a variety of vehicles or advanced on foot. Somali fighters in organized platoons and squads of six or seven fanned out to buildings, doorways, walled areas, and trees to avoid the AH-6s and MH-60Ls. This raid was a major thrust into the heart of Aideed territory, so there was no problem getting more fighters to take on the Americans. Giumale possessed mass of numbers and territorial advantages that could secure a victory.

SNA supporters started to shoot at the TFR elements and crowds appeared around the assault force and the chalks. Each of the chalks was about a block from the target building except for Eversmann's Chalk 4. His chalk was two blocks away since the helicopter had dropped him one block too far. The Rangers in the chalks used abandoned vehicles and other cover to avoid enemy snipers and to return fire from a more protected position. Somali AK-47, grenade, and other fire kept the Americans busy, but the crowds did not reach the target house. However, helicopter crews saw individuals with RPGs heading to the area. Aideed's supporters mixed with the crowd and fired at the chalks, helicopters, and ground convoy. SNA gunmen and others also used the crowd as a shield against return fire by the Americans.

The assault force had captured Salad, Awale, and 24 SNA members. Delta members "flex-cuffed" the prisoners, and awaited McKnight in the ground convoy for evacuation. TFR personnel guarded the prisoners in the building's courtyard to better control them and avoid putting them on the street where they could be shot. The Delta troops, Rangers, and helicopter pilots awaited the signal "Laurie" to begin the evacuation to the airport. With that command, the Rangers in the chalks were to collapse their positions to near the target building to exit the area. Miller called his Delta squadron commander and stated: "We're ready to get out of Dodge." TFR had accomplished the mission in about 15 minutes with 20 Delta members who had rushed into the building. With the exception of Blackburn's injury, the raid was a big success.

"Super 61's Going Down"

SNA militiamen had already arrived around the Olympic Hotel area and had started to move throughout Mogadishu to the raid site. Armed with automatic firearms and RPGs, the SNA could catch the Americans in a deadly grip, but first they needed to neutralize their foe's major advantage, the helicopters. An MH-60L was not an easy target to hit. The helicopters mostly flew empty, but the MH-60Ls had two crew chiefs operating the

OCTOBER 3 1993

1540hrs Raid on Olympic Hotel commences

OCTOBER 3 1993

1555hrs Snatch operation completed

miniguns and many had SOF snipers onboard. If the AH-6s caught sight of an RPG-armed Somali, they would attack the insurgent instantly. Reports to Garrison nevertheless indicated the helicopters were facing many Somalis firing their RPGs. The 160th SOAR pilots took their helicopters to altitudes of about 200ft to provide fire support, a position that also made them a target for small-arms fire.

Wolcott, in Super 61, navigated the Black Sea neighborhood at less than 100 knots and tried to make the flight path erratic to avoid flying into an ambush, and to confuse any RPG operator. The pilot moved from a northeast direction toward the target building. Despite these efforts, his helicopter started to receive ground fire. Wolcott and other 160th SOAR pilots were aware of the September 25 shoot-down of Courage 53, the QRF UH-60, and the potential threat of Somali RPG fire. He and another Black Hawk crew provided fire support for TFR forces on the ground, but the numbers of RPG smoke trails started to increase around the target building. At about 1620hrs, a single, fatal RPG smashed into Wolcott's Black Hawk. Wolcott tried to control the damaged MH-60, but it was no use – the helicopter went into an uncontrolled spin.

Some of the Rangers in the chalks watched the MH-60L spiral down near Marehan Road. Wolcott could do nothing but try to land his stricken craft and save his passengers and crew. Helicopter pilots, the JOC, and others heard the MH-60's distress call of "Super 61's going down." The helicopter crashed northeast of the target building about three blocks, or roughly a few hundred yards away. The Black Hawk now lay crumpled as a shattered hulk between Marehan Road and Freedom Avenue. Part of the helicopter sat against a building wall, near a courtyard that had caved in. Garrison's staff was stunned. The unthinkable had happened. The SNA had now caught Garrison's men in a very vulnerable position. TFR's advantage of speed and surprise to accomplish the mission was gone. If Aideed's supporters could reach the helicopter crash before the TFR forces, then the SNA might take American prisoners, or worse. Alive or dead, the SNA would make a public spectacle of the crew to the news media if they got hold of them. Aideed could use the news coverage to transform a relatively disinterested American public into an opposing force in Congress, pushing for a withdrawal of American support in Somalia.

Garrison had lost the initiative in the raid and that initiative was slowly shifting to the Somalis. The mission's character had altered dramatically. The simple call to take Aideed's lieutenants had now changed to a rescue of the downed Black Hawk.

Super 61's crash required an immediate change in plans. Instead of getting ready to move out to return to base immediately, Garrison and the TFR planners now had to reach Super 61 fast. The contingency plans included three elements: land the CSAR helicopter immediately, call up the QRF, and get the Rangers from the chalks and any available Delta from the assault force moving toward the crash site. The CSAR helicopter – Super 68 – was soon at the scene of the crash site. A combination of five Delta, seven Ranger, and two Air Force pararescue and one combat controller were ready on Super 68. The Delta members and Rangers would secure the area. The Air Force pararescue and a Ranger medic provided medical support for any wounded crew members while the Air Force combat controller coordinated fire support.

The QRF would require time to organize and move to the crash site. Montgomery's QRF was standing by, but even though they were only a few miles away, a road journey might take time. Any QRF convoy would have to penetrate into an area under hostile fire. Company C was the current alert force and would attempt to move toward the crash site from their base – near the former Somali National University compound next to the American embassy – to the Black Sea area.

The closest TFR ground force was Chalk 2 with Di Tomasso's men. He was less than 400 yards away. He saw many Somalis trying to move toward Super 61, which was about two blocks parallel to his position, and he knew he had to get to the position before the enemy. His Rangers started moving out, but he left a few members of the chalk to secure the area. Two other chalks also started to move out to the crash site. The only chalk that remained was Eversmann's chalk 4. He would remain in place and await pick-up by McKnight, who would secure the prisoners first and then go to Super 61's position. Eversmann moved toward the target building after he heard the codeword for extraction. McKnight was moving toward the target building.

Super 68's CSAR crew prepared for action. Super 61's wingman, Super 62, was over Wolcott's crash site providing suppressing fire to keep the crowds away. No one in TFR knew if Super 61's crew and passengers were alive or dead, but the TFR pilots did not want to take a chance of repeating the fate of the Courage 53 crew for Super 61 – Somalis had mutilated that crews' bodies a week earlier. Before the CSAR force could reach the crash site, an MH-6, Star 41, made an incredible landing behind Wolcott's helicopter tail rotor. They attempted to rescue the wounded crew. The MH-6's rotating main rotors barely fit in the street, but it set down a half block

OCTOBER 3
1993

1620hrs
"Super 61" Black
Hawk shot down
by RPG

from the MH-60 at 1624hrs. The Star 41 crew pulled in two wounded Delta members while Super 68 personnel prepared to fast-rope. One of the MH-6 crew members steadied the helicopter while firing a weapon to keep back the gathering Somali crowd. The other pilot had left the helicopter to help the wounded into the Little Bird. Di Tomasso arrived at the crash site to witness the event. Star 41 left with the Delta members for the airport. Unfortunately, one of the wounded died.

The CSAR teams dropped into the Super 61 site. While the SOF members left the MH-60L, an RPG struck Super 68 behind the cargo area in the main rotor section as the last person left the helicopter. The pilot kept the helicopter steady, as best as possible, until this person touched the ground safely. The crew thought Super 68 would end up like Super 61, since the RPG hit the engine area, which was smoking badly. Shrapnel had damaged the main rotor blades. Fortunately, the crew nursed the limping aircraft back to the airport. The crew immediately got into a spare MH-60L to return to the battle. There was little chance that Super 68 would operate for the rest of the mission.

The CSAR team found Wolcott and his co-pilot, Chief Warrant Officer Donovan Brilley, dead. Both pilot and co-pilot appeared to have pushed Super 61's nose down intentionally to take the brunt of the impact force. This action spared the passengers further injury. Wolcott's body lay wedged in the wreckage and the team could not remove it. Somali small-arms fire and grenades pelted the MH-60L, but the medics and other TFR personnel helped Super 61's two hurt crew chiefs and two other Delta snipers who were on the helicopter. Arriving Delta members established a security perimeter, with Di Tomasso's Rangers, around the helicopter. The medics created a casualty collection point (CCP) in the area where the Black Hawk fuselage had crashed. The area provided temporary protection in which the medics could treat any wounded. Other elements from the chalks and Delta assault team finally reached the crash site area at 1726hrs. There were 99 TFR members at the crash site and the Somalis surrounded them.

The 10th Mountain Division QRF could call on air support from AH-1 Cobra attack helicopters like this one. This Cobra provides direct fire against clan militiamen who are fighting with American forces near American Embassy in Mogadishu. (DoD)

Ground Convoy to the Rescue

Once the Delta forces had taken and secured their detainees, McKnight heard the signal "Laurie," informing him that the assault forces had taken their targets and they were ready to get out. McKnight pushed on to get the prisoners from the target building on Hawlwadig Road. The Rangers and Delta started to get the prisoners ready to move out. McKnight had decided to ship Blackburn back to the airport immediately. He received approval, by the C2 helicopter, to split up the convoy. Three HMMWVs, with Blackburn, would return to the base.

The pick-up zone for the Delta assault force was also under increasingly heavy fire from the SNA and others. McKnight's new orders were to gather all of the prisoners and Americans and to proceed to the first crash site, less the three HMMWVs transporting Blackburn. McKnight would simply add the other Rangers, Delta, CSAR team, and the wounded crew from Super 61 into his column. McKnight asked for help from the QRF. During the 30 minutes it took to load the prisoners in the vehicles, the Somali fire intensified. A Somali gunman shot a HMMWV Mk 19 gunner, who died. The convoy continued to draw fire from all directions and the Rangers responded in force. An RPG struck and destroyed one of the 5-ton trucks. McKnight had suffered more casualties. The convoy finally left the target building, but the Somalis started hitting the vehicles with small-arms fire and RPGs. McKnight's convoy consisted of about 75 Americans and prisoners.

The three-HMMWV vehicle convoy tried to return to the airport through the same route it had used earlier. Rangers fought Somalis every step of the way. While operating a machine gun mounted on a HMMWV, a Ranger received a bullet in the head and died. Fortunately, the convoy made it through to the TFR base, but the trip had been costly. The soldiers at the airport were getting ready too – many wanted to go out to help their comrades.

OCTOBER 3
1993

1630hrs
QRF notified
of rescue
mission

Mogadishu International Airport was the base for TFR operations throughout the city. It also served as an entry port for critical supplies and personnel arriving and departing Somalia. AC-130Hs would refuel and rearm at this airport to support UN activities. (DoD)

Meanwhile, McKnight was having problems navigating the streets north and east of the target building. The C2 helicopter tried to keep the column on track to the first crash site, but the convoy got lost and was driving around Mogadishu attempting to avoid barricades and ambushes. After the convoy had picked up the passengers and the remaining Rangers and Delta, it had proceeded south for a few blocks then north toward another main city artery, the Armed Forces Road. Unfortunately, confusing directions, enemy fire, smoke, and blockades made the simple route complex. McKnight and the vehicles missed the crash site; they were about two blocks from Super 61 and the rest of the TFR elements. The convoy headed north to try to reach the site again, but took a wrong turn and started to drive south toward the target building and the Olympic Hotel instead of Wolcott's position. The area was now full of SNA militia, and their supporters were ready when the convoy reappeared. After passing the Olympic Hotel, the McKnight convoy had to make a U-turn to head north again. Out of the original nine vehicles, the convoy had seven left – another vehicle had become disabled due to enemy fire. More Rangers were dead or wounded. Garrison ordered the convoy to return to the airport amid reports from McKnight that he had taken too many casualties and was combat-ineffective. McKnight thought he would be more of a burden than a help at Super 61. After moving a few blocks, the convoy passed Wolcott's crash site again heading north toward the Armed Forces Road. Throughout the journey, McKnight's trucks and HMMWVs took fire from both sides of the street as they ran a gauntlet of fire.

Despite having helicopters to guide the US column through Mogadishu, the smoke and confusion created conditions in which drivers got lost easily. Earlier, the trucks displayed on their roofs large high-visibility orange identification panels, which the C2 helicopter could track. Even these panels were difficult to see after firefights developed. McKnight had to set off a purple smoke marker to identify his position to the helicopters on one occasion. Once told to leave the area and return to base, the lead command HMMWV, with McKnight, started moving ahead. Before reaching Armed Forces Road, McKnight's vehicle and the remaining convoy started to lose contact and became separated. Fortunately, McKnight and the convoy were quickly reunited and they proceeded down the road and finally south to K-4 Circle.

During his return journey, McKnight linked up with a group of 27 TFR personnel from the airport in seven HMMWVs, which Garrison had organized as a relief column for a second helicopter crash, Super 64 (see below). The relief column was formed by administrative personnel, cooks, support and maintenance troops, other Rangers available for duty, and the men that had retrieved Blackburn. The rescue force moved out into the battle on the same path as the original ground convoy and became involved in a fierce fight near the K-4 Circle. While trying to reach the site, they faced a barricade of burning tires that blocked their path. McKnight ordered them back to the airport, since it appeared that they could not break through the barricade.

Given the level of Somali opposition, McKnight's relief column would have faced a serious challenge getting to Super 61's position. Before leaving together for the airport, McKnight ordered the prisoners and wounded placed in the undamaged HMMWVs for the completion of their return trip.

McKnight lost one HMMVV and two 5-ton trucks. One truck, carrying the Somali prisoners, lost its driver when a RPG struck and decapitated him. Scores of wounded Americans and Somalis were in the vehicles. Every Ranger and Delta member returned fire with all available weapons. With his soldiers running low on ammunition, McKnight's force would have had a very difficult task to break through to the crash site to reinforce the men at Super 61. During the loading of prisoners at the target building, the two loops around the Black Sea area, and the return to the airport, half of McKnight's men had received wounds. Some of the soldiers had suffered mortal wounds and three of the 24 prisoners also died. At least Salad and Awale were still alive.

Super 64 Goes Down

Chief Warrant Officer Michael Durant, in Super 64, had earlier delivered Steele, Perino, and their Rangers to their blocking position. Without any more passengers, Super 64 had been in a holding pattern waiting to provide assistance to the ground forces. When Super 61 hit the ground due to the RPG strike, the C2 Black Hawk ordered Durant to replace Wolcott's position. Durant had the task of supplying minigun suppressive fire against the growing hostile mob of Somalis moving toward the Super 61 crash site. Additionally, the crew chiefs on board Super 64 also opened fire on anyone trying to kill the D-boys and Rangers who headed toward the helicopter crash. The C2 Black Hawk and EP-3 watched the TFR soldiers move across several blocks in the Black Sea area, trying to make it to Wolcott's position. Durant knew that Super 61 was down and that Super 68 had suffered a damaging RPG hit too. He moved into position over Wolcott's crash site to assume a "low CAP" (combat air patrol) and respond to requests for close air support.

Lightning struck twice. At 1640hrs, one of the many Somali RPGs loosed off against the TFR forces struck Super 64's tail rotor area. The helicopter seemed to operate properly and Durant was still able to maneuver. Durant attempted to fly toward the airport. Within a few minutes, however, the tail rotor assembly fell apart and control became impossible. Durant's craft was leaking oil and smoking heavily. If the helicopter could only stay together for about three to four minutes, then Durant could put down at the airport like Super 68 or at least get to a more friendly area under American or UN control. Instead, Super 64 started to gyrate wildly and his wingman, in Super 62, along with the airborne C2 helicopter, advised him to set the helicopter down immediately. The MH-60 was about to crash. Durant's helicopter descended 100ft straight into the ground. The Black Hawk came to rest southwest of Super 61's position, about a half mile away. The crew had taken several precautions to reduce the chance of flipping over by shutting off the twin engines. The Black Hawk went down near a collection of shacks, some damaged in the impact. Pieces of the helicopter flew in all directions and caused casualties among the local residents.

OCTOBER 3
1993

1640hrs
"Super 64" hit in
tail rotor and
crash-lands

OCTOBER 3
1993

1700hrs
First QRF units
move out to
assemble at
New Port

PREVIOUS PAGES
When Super 64 crashed, there was little that Major General William Garrison could do to rescue Michael Durant and his crew. Garrison arranged for the QFR and sent a TFR rescue force, but both failed to break through. Two Delta snipers, Gary Gordon and Randy Shughart, volunteered to help the crew until TFR could mount another rescue. Against a surging Somali crowd, the Americans mounted a desperate defense. With two helicopter losses and increased RPG threats, Garrison's staff could not send any more helicopters into the area. Gordon and Shughart could not hold out indefinitely against overwhelming odds and soon fell. Durant's crew also died at the hands of the SNA and their supporters. Durant would survive, and Aideed released him days later after using him as a propaganda tool for the SNA. Congress awarded both Gordon and Shughart the Congressional Medal of Honor for their bravery and sacrifice.

Super 62 flew over Durant's location. There were signs of life – even from the air, helicopter crews saw movement in the cockpit. The four-man crew had survived the hard landing, although they were injured, and were trying to get out of the wreckage. The area's residents had seen the crash and a crowd surged toward Super 64. The Americans had destroyed part of their homes and had injured some local people, so many Somalis wanted revenge. Other than the two-man crew, Super 62 had crew chiefs operating the miniguns and three Delta snipers. Some of the Little Bird crews also volunteered to land nearby and allow one of the two crew members to secure the area until reinforcements came. The increasing mob size, the distance from the nearest ground support, the loss of three helicopters, and the increasing volume of Somali small-arms fire convinced the C2 helicopter controllers to stop any attempt at rescue. They did not need another aircraft casualty and more TFR members killed or wounded. Still, many helicopter crews and others felt a rescue was needed fast, especially with the Somali crowd ready to descend on Durant.

Master Sergeant Gary I. Gordon and Sergeant First Class Randy D. Shughart, two Delta snipers on Super 62, insisted on helping the Super 64 crew. Knowing that their own rescue would be problematic with an angry crowd surrounding the crash site, Gordon and Shughart pressed for an immediate authorization to help Durant. The C2 helicopter operators granted their request after they queried both snipers about the situation and recognition that they might be on their own for a long time.

Durant's crash site was in a neighborhood of numerous nondescript buildings and shacks. Super 62 was able to hover low enough for the two snipers to drop 5ft out of the helicopter instead of fast-roping. They would have to move north, less than 100 yards, to reach Durant. AH-6s had arrived to provide fire support to keep the Somalis away from Super 64. The two snipers had trouble picking their way through the area, but moved toward Super 64 with the aid of a smoke marker dropped by a helicopter. Time was on the Somalis' side. SNA militia mass, despite the TFR helicopters, would engulf the crash site along with Gordon and Shughart. Another danger also lurked – more Somalis armed with RPGs advanced near the area ready to strike another helicopter.

The hostile mob lurched toward Durant's helicopter. Gordon and Shughart had helped some of the crew members as best as they could, but they had to secure the area around the downed helicopter. All were injured and required immediate aid. The two Delta snipers had lifted Durant out of the helicopter and put him outside and to the rear of the MH-60L. They also took out the rest of the crew. Durant had suffered a compound fracture to his upper right leg and a severe back injury, so he could hardly move.

Despite intense enemy fire, the pair of snipers kept the mob at bay with accurate and disciplined shooting. Durant had an MP5K submachine gun and protected his crew and Gordon and Shughart's rear. The surging crowd made it increasingly difficult for the Americans to stop their movement. Supporting helicopter crews were shooting M16s, miniguns, and other weapons to try to stop the crowd, but it was not enough. Durant had only

President William J. Clinton awarded the Congressional Medal of Honor (posthumously) to the widows of Sergeant First Class Randall D. Shughart (left) and Master Sergeant Gary I. Gordon (center) on May 23, 1994. Gordon and Shughart provided sniper fire during an assault on a building and at both helicopter crash sites and they attempted to rescue Super 64's crew. They died on October 3, 1993. (DoD)

two clips of ammunition and soon ran out. First Gordon, then Shughart, died from gunshots, along with the three other Super 64 Black Hawk crew members. Shughart, before he met his end, had asked Durant if there were any weapons left in Super 64. Durant mentioned that there were M16s for the crew chiefs. Shughart returned and gave Durant a CAR-15, Gordon's weapon. Durant had heard Gordon yell out earlier that he had been hit, and then there was silence. Shughart put up a defense until Somali small-arms fire overcame him too. Durant had used all of his rounds for the CAR-15; he only had his sidearm, a pistol, to defend himself, but it seemed hopeless. Somalis soon surrounded Durant. There was no way out. One man smashed Durant's face with a rifle butt, and others beat him. Despite having a pistol, Durant had decided not to resist since he thought he was dead anyway, but it was not to be.

Yousef Dahir Mo'alim, a neighborhood SNA leader, had decided to spare Durant and claimed him as a captive for Aideed. No one was to beat Durant anymore. Before moving Durant, the Somalis removed the Personnel Locator System, a device to locate crew members in a search-and-rescue mission, from him and the other pilot. Despite being saved from the mob, Durant needed treatment for his leg and back, and the Somalis did get him medical help. The US pilot made a valuable prize for SNA leadership to parade before the global media, and he was forced to make a propaganda video. Aideed held Durant captive for 11 days, before he was eventually released to the International Red Cross. Congress posthumously awarded Gordon and Shughart America's highest decoration, the Medal of Honor, the first given since the Vietnam War.

Meanwhile, Garrison and TFR had no idea what had happened to Durant, the crew, and the snipers. RPG fire filled the airspace around the crash site. The C2 Black Hawk ordered the remaining aircrews out – flying was getting too dangerous around Super 64. Star 41 attempted a rescue attempt similar to that performed at the Super 61 crash. They set down their MH-6 in the hope that a crew member would reach the Little Bird, but no one could escape the Aideed supporters. Super 62 had kept up their fire support for Gordon and Shughart, but it had become a magnet for RPG fire too. The helicopter's luck ran out when an RPG struck the Black Hawk under its right minigun position. The remaining Delta sniper in the helicopter replaced a wounded crew chief, whose leg had been taken off by the RPG blast, as the minigun operator. The co-pilot also suffered wounds and was out of the fight. The pilot thought they were also going down into the Somali mob, but he managed to fly to the New Port area and safety. Garrison ordered Super 68 to fly to the New Port to transfer casualties from Super 62 to the airport for medical aid.

Garrison could not immediately help Super 64, although a QRF rescue team readied itself to break through to the site. Rangers and Delta troops had reached Super 61, but did not have the means to reach Gordon and Shughart. Aideed supporters had pinned them down. McKnight's convoy and the earlier deployed Ranger relief column only had enough capability to head back to the airport. McKnight needed to get medical attention for the wounded, turn over the prisoners, acquire more ammunition, and find replacements. The only replacements available would have to come from the dwindling number of TFR, the three companies from Montgomery's contingent, and the UN. Gathering these men would take time to plan, organize, and execute.

Company C, from the 10th Mountain Division had received notification to get ready at 1630hrs to support TFR as soon as possible. Soldiers carried LAWs and AT-4s. The AT-4 was a single-shot 84mm antitank weapon that soldiers can use to destroy vehicles or punch through walls. Company C and the 2nd Battalion's tactical command post left the compound. The QRF drove to the airport with 150 soldiers in 12 HMMWVs and nine 2½-ton trucks at 1710hrs. Along with the infantry company, the force included an

The major source of fire support for ground transportation came from HMMWV-mounted .50cal machine guns or the Mk 19 automatic grenade launcher on this vehicle. This HMMWV in Somalia could fire 40mm grenades from the Mk 19 to suppress SNA attacks. (DoD)

engineer squad and a medical team with the battalion surgeon. It also took extra ammunition, about 50 percent more than the normal load.

When the QRF was ready to go to Durant's crash site, it left at 1735hrs. Here was the only independent QRF effort to rescue the Super 64 force. Garrison's staff believed that they could initially handle the situation with only Super 61 down, but with Durant's Black Hawk lying in the dirt the situation was beyond their capability. The 10th Mountain Division force headed north on Via Lenin, but met stiff resistance at the K-4 Circle from SNA militia and others. The QRF made a request for air support from the QRF's AH-1s, and a firefight ensued that lasted for half an hour. Somali opposition was too much to overcome and the QRF could not proceed any further.

Colonel Lawrence Casper, commanding the QRF force, ordered the column back to the airport. Their attempt to help rescue Durant was problematic anyway, and the Somali crowd was overrunning Gordon and Shughart's Super 64 position at this time. The QRF would remain at the airport for another attempted rescue, but Montgomery would also have to activate Companies A and B to support the rescue efforts. Both were ready to go into Mogadishu. He would also need armored vehicles; small-arms fire and RPGs had torn up many of the TFR HMMWVs and trucks. Garrison and Montgomery did not have any other type of transportation. The only forces with tanks and APCs to protect TFR were UNOSOM II forces.

Securing Super 61

Lieutenant Di Tomasso was one of the first TFR ground elements to reach Super 61's crash site. He started directing his M60 machine gun team to set up near a corner, north of his position to the crashed helicopter, to stop the Somali crowd that had paralleled his movement toward Super 61. He sent other Rangers northeast of the MH-60's location. They, along with the CSAR team, would eventually create a defensive position near Super 61's hulk. At least the TFR members could use the buildings to entrench themselves. As he reached Wolcott's location, Di Tomasso had watched the CSAR team drop into the area. Di Tomasso also called for the team members he had left at the original chalk position to start moving toward his position. Once that team reached the Super 61 area, Di Tomasso ordered the Rangers to set up at the southwestern corner of the defense perimeter. He sent an M60 crew to shore up the northeastern defense position to ward off any Somalis that might outflank him.

Despite efforts to secure the perimeter, the CSAR and Rangers came under continual attack from Somali militia and irregular forces. Defending the area entailed a huge expenditure of ammunition. The Delta members and Rangers faced enraged Somalis inching forward toward all American positions. The mass of fire from the SNA had also taken its toll, inflicting additional TFR casualties. For example,

UN peacekeepers found all types of small arms throughout Somalia. Many weapons were AK-47s, while others dated from much earlier conflicts. Although many weapons needed repair, they could still operate and kill or wound rival clan members or peacekeepers. (DoD)

Perino's chalk section, which had advanced to the crash site, would eventually suffer ten casualties out of 13 men. Other groups faced similar conditions. The wounded along with the able-bodied had to beat back the waves of Somalis.

Despite their spirited effort, the TFR soldiers were in a perilous situation. TFR forces had prepared for a quick daylight mission only; removing the 24 SNA captives should have taken a few minutes' drive back to Mogadishu airport. The Delta troops and Rangers did not expect to fight a major engagement. Garrison now faced a completely different mission. From being a raid, the operation had radically changed to an immediate combat rescue. Unfortunately, few available resources remained. McKnight's ground convoy had suffered numerous killed and wounded. The 160th SOAR suffered several damaged MH-60Ls and had two been destroyed. The TFR contingent had used up their contingency force and now faced a major fight with hundreds of Somali fighters. Water was also becoming an issue, since few soldiers took any into battle. Availability of medical supplies became critical too. Time was getting short; darkness would soon follow. The missing night-vision goggles would have provided superior sighting to identify targets for the AH-6s and return fire against the Somalis. Worst, all TFR and QRF attempts to rescue the Americans at Super 61 had been fruitless. Garrison would need to expedite his efforts to call on the UN and the QRF.

The soldiers at Super 61 would have to wait for any rescue. They could only rely on their own tactical skills, leadership, and firepower to hold back the Black Sea residents. If Garrison could resupply them with ammunition, water, and medical supplies, then they might hold out. The Americans still had one major advantage – they could still call on their helicopters. Although the 160th SOAR had sustained two devastating losses, they possessed one major advantage, the AH-6s. The Little Birds continued to demonstrate their superior firepower during the day and would perform even better in the night. The QRF brought their AH-1F Cobra attack helicopters too. These attack helicopters could also operate at night with their miniguns and other weapons. Furthermore, Garrison could undertake an aerial resupply mission with his MH-60s.

Mounting Another Rescue

The Super 61 crash site now contained a sizeable contingent of CSAR, Delta, and Rangers protecting the area. The soldiers spread out along a two-block area on Marehan Road in a reverse, upside down "L" position. At the top of the "L" was Super 61's battered fuselage. The original rescuers had set up a good spot to observe and protect the wounded. That position included the wounded helicopter crew, the CSAR element, and some of the Chalk 2 Rangers from Di Tomasso's contingent. Moving down Marehan Road was Miller and some of the Delta assault force. They had established a fire team and headquarters section. Proceeding south was Perino and another Delta team. On the second block, a Delta team prepared to defend the area next to a building sheltering Steele with more Rangers. TFR had spread out along the road, making it difficult to concentrate fire to defend the helicopter.

OCTOBER 3 1993

1726hrs Final elements of assault force reach Super 61

The QRF seemed to offer the best hope of rescuing the TFR forces around Super 61. Garrison did not know the fate of Super 64 and he would need to send someone to search the area to ascertain the helicopter crew's status. A benefit of using the QRF was that they had trained with the UNOSOM II forces. Although not entirely familiar with each country's capabilities, Montgomery's soldiers did at least try to understand their operations. On October 3, the QRF's Company A had scheduled a training mission with the Pakistanis and Malaysians near the airport to practice taking certain checkpoints from the clans in the city. Moving by helicopter, Company A waited for the training mission, but it did not take place. The Americans returned to their compound at 1100hrs.

Now Garrison had to come up with a plan to remove his TFR forces. He could rely on his fellow Americans, both Montgomery's and his remaining Rangers and Delta. Fortunately, Montgomery held a dual hat as second-in-command of UNOSOM II troops and the top commander of American forces assigned to the UN. There were four countries with sufficient combat capability and transportation to assist – the Italians, Indians, Pakistanis, and Malaysians all had armored vehicles. The Italians and Indians needed approval from their capitals to launch the rescue mission, but the Pakistanis and Malaysians were ready to act straight away. Time was of the essence, so the plan was to meet the two Malaysian mechanized infantry companies and one Pakistani armored company at the New Port.

Montgomery's QRF became an invaluable resource for Garrison. Company C was already at the TFR base camp. Company A was the next-best ready force. The battalion scout platoon, psychological operations team, and other support elements prepared to go with Company A to the New Port. Company B was another source of reinforcements for TFR. Transportation limited the time and ability to get the soldiers from the university compound to the airport and then to the rendezvous point, however.

Company A was ready to move out around 1700hrs. The only information that the company leadership had received was that the Somalis had shot down a helicopter and that the company was supposed to support Company C, which was in a firefight trying to break through to the downed MH-60 near the K-4 Circle. As Company A checked their equipment, they heard heavy gunfire from the city over the battalion radio link. Garrison's staff had by now requested Company C to withdraw to the airport, since it was closer to their position. Likewise, the battalion received orders to move Companies A and B to the airport too.

The combined convoy consisted of 15 HMMWVs and trucks. Company A moved first; Company B would travel later when HMMWVs and the trucks became available. The convoy took a circuitous route to reach the airport that lasted 45 minutes. Company B would travel at night. Mogadishu did not have streetlights, and putting on their vehicles' headlights would also attracted undue attention from the Somalis, so drivers had to rely on night-vision goggles to travel the route.

TFR planners created a plan to break through to the downed helicopters at 1900hrs. Companies A and C, along with a TFR contingent, would drive

to the New Port. Some of this force would then transfer to 32 Malaysian Condor APCs, and four Pakistani M48s would escort the rescue force, which consisted of about 70 vehicles in total. The column would first move east then north to National Street, then west toward the Olympic Hotel. From that location, elements of the relief column could continue to both crash sites. Once the American and UN forces rescued or recovered the TFR members, the convoy would return to the New Port.

The QRF and TFR units were under no illusion that they would not have to fight their way into the city. The plan called for Company A, as the main attack force, to break through to the encircled Rangers and Delta at the first crash site. The battalion tactical command post and Company C would follow. Company C's soldiers would search Durant's crash position to look for any signs of the crew and snipers. All agreed that they would recover all Americans, dead or alive. The Americans were to leave nothing for the Somalis; soldiers would destroy Super 61 and 64.

The Pakistani tanks would lead off the rescue. Lieutenant Colonel Bill David, the QRF battalion commander, was in a HMMWV following the tanks, with Company A in Condors. The convoy also had a HMMWV frontline ambulance, and volunteers from TFR. Rangers and other SOF from TFR made up a contingent of seven armored HMMWVs at the rear of the column. Some of Company A's personnel had orders to stay behind at the airport to supplement TFR. Company B, when moved to the New Port loading area, would become part of the rescue force's reserve contingent.

Task Force (TF) 2-25, the "Ravens," a part of the QRF aerial contingent, would provide cover for the convoy to National Street. Once elements of the column crossed north of National Street toward Super 61, the 160th SOAR's AH-6s would watch over the rescue force. OH-58s and AH-1s were available to support the Delta and Rangers, but Garrison had earlier declined since there were problems managing the airspace around the crash sites. Too many helicopters in a confined area might create issues, with AH-6s and AH-1s trying to make simultaneous firing passes at the same target. An OH-58D was already airborne scouting the rescue columns path. OH-58s would locate targets at night with their sensors, and then use a laser to illuminate them for the AH-1Fs.

Company A arrived at the port area around 2030hrs. The QRF and TFR movement from the airport toward the New Port was slow. Vehicles carrying the Americans to the assembly area jammed the roads. A simple drive of about a mile took 30 minutes. By 2100hrs, TFR had suffered 13 seriously wounded and three killed at the Super 61 crash site, so the rescue column needed to move out soon.

Once assembled in a large parking lot at the port, the loading onto the Condors started. Before the Americans could depart, they had to resolve a language issue. Not all Malaysians spoke English. Fortunately, the Americans and Malaysians exchanged information on how to operate the doors and weapons in the APCs (each Condor had a 20mm cannon and light machine gun manned by Malaysian gunners). Some Americans called them "coffins on wheels." Malaysian infantry also accompanied the

Condors, although the Americans explained that they did not need the extra soldiers for the operation.

Company A was composed of three platoons. The first platoon contained infantry, mortar and fire-support elements, and a medic. An engineer squad and medic accompanied the second platoon. Accompanying the last platoon was another medic. The first platoon used three Condors; the other two platoons only had two Condors each. A forward medical treatment team also went with Company A.

The American, Pakistani, and Malaysian officers conferred on the route. The Pakistani tank commander disagreed about his role and about the distance that his tanks had to travel into the Black Sea area. He was under orders not to lead the convoy. After negotiations, he agreed to move out with the column. Pakistani tankers would lead the column up to National Street and then allow the Malaysian Condors to spearhead the American and UN procession into the contested area.

At about 2323hrs, the QRF rolled out of the New Port to rescue the surrounded TFR forces. Information was sketchy about the conditions near Super 61. David had to rush the combined American and UN forces out toward the crash sites.

TFR Hunkers Down for the Night

Aideed supporters and local residents sniped at US soldiers around the crash site all afternoon and night. Soldiers had removed Kevlar floorboards from Super 61 as shielding. Kevlar is the same material used in helmets and parts of the soldiers' body armor, and it provided some protection for the wounded Americans and the medics in the improvised CCP near the shattered MH-60. Earlier attempts to move the wounded to a more secure location near the crash had failed because of the increasing gunfire from the Somalis. Under the cover of darkness, the TFR members finally moved the wounded into a

OCTOBER 3
1993

2323hrs
QRF begins
rescue mission

During UNOSOM operations, Marines conducted several security sweeps in Mogadishu to look for weapons. In Mogadishu, many UN forces concentrated on Aideed's activities. This Aideed follower surrenders after taking heavy fire into a weapons cantonment area during a search for illegal weapons by American personnel. (DoD)

The QRF rescue convoy departing from the New Port used UN Condor APCs manned by Malaysian troops. The vehicles filled up with litters and wounded once they reached the Super 61 location. Somalis destroyed two Condors in the mission. (DoD)

After the October 3–4 raid, Clinton ordered additional American forces, including tanks and APCs, into Somalia. This training exercise in Mogadishu practices extraction of casualties into APCs. Unfortunately, this armored emphasis came too late for TFR. (DoD)

building. They had to create a safe evacuation route in case the Somalis overran the area, so used an explosive charge to blow an escape hole through a wall into another house.

Despite positioning themselves in houses and walled areas, the Americans had continued to suffer casualties. Medics rigged up intravenous (IV) solution bags to the wounded. Medical supplies of all types started to get dangerously low; the medics ran out of morphine and they had to ration the IV bags. The Super 61 wreck had become the main attraction for AK-47 fire, grenades, and RPG missiles. Soldiers earlier had witnessed crowds of combatants and non-combatants milling around the area. Women and children had weapons, from AK-47s to knives. Others pointed out American positions for other armed Somalis to fire upon. Some armed men fired from behind non-combatants as they advanced near the TFR soldiers. Fortunately, AH-6s, working in pairs, continually supported the surrounded Americans. They played the major part in holding back the Somalis throughout the night. The Air Force combat controllers on the ground directed the Little Birds onto Somali positions, using infrared (IR) pointers to illuminate enemy positions. The Little Birds only returned to base to rearm and refuel.

While David prepared to move out of the New Port area, Super 61 rescuers continued to suffer. The D-boys and Rangers at the northern crash site had been under continuous fire for hours. In his area, Di Tomasso and the CSAR team had to contend with two killed and 11 wounded, three of the wounded being in a serious condition. Other TFR positions were also struggling to resist. All along Marehan Road the Americans started to run out of ammunition and water. Soldiers gave any remaining water to the wounded. One of Di Tomasso's men did find a water spigot that had provided some water, although some soldiers were concerned about its cleanliness.

One MH-60 conducted a resupply mission. Garrison knew that the Delta and Rangers could not hold out without support, so Super 66 dropped ammunition, water, and medical supplies to an area marked by an IR strobe at about 1910hrs. TFR soldiers scrambled to get the packages dropped down the middle of Marehan Road. The Somalis focused their fire on the helicopter, but it survived the attack – one crew member received a wound and Super 66 sustained damage to its transmission, so did not fly again that day. Fears that the Somalis might down another Black Hawk ended all thoughts of another resupply mission or a much-needed medical evacuation for the critical wounded. The combined QRF, TFR, and UN rescue force was forming and should soon start its breakthrough efforts anyway.

Even though the Americans received these supplies, distribution of the ammunition and medical provisions would not be easy. Steele's Rangers were too distant from the resupply effort and his men did not get any ammunition or medical supplies. His soldiers were getting low on ammunition; some only had half of the supply that they brought with them a few hours earlier. Another problem about the dispersed TFR positions concerned the ability to get support from the AH-6s. Pilots had to take extra measures to ensure they were not hitting friendly positions. If the TFR soldiers had consolidated into a single location, close air support coordination might have improved. Regardless, the AH-6s continued to attack the Somalis.

The Rangers and Delta had spread out along a two-block area and they were under fire from locations as close as next door to their positions. Some SNA supporters threw grenades behind a common wall. Somali fighters also had time to deploy heavier weapons to the crash site. The SNA brought up some of their technical trucks with heavy machine guns and recoilless rifles. The Rangers and Delta kept pressing Garrison's staff to get the QRF moving faster.

The Somali opposition, emboldened by the helicopter shoot-downs and stopping the reinforcement efforts, now had a chance of wiping out the Americans. Giumale had succeeded in surrounding and cutting off the TFR rescue force. Although he had a distinct advantage over the Americans, he was still wary of their technological strengths. He could still communicate by radio to his forces, but there was some concern that the Americans could intercept and decipher his messages. Instead, he had to use written orders moved by runners. This approach slowed down his actions, but reinforcements from throughout Mogadishu still streamed to the crash site. Giumale only controlled the SNA militia; irregular forces and ordinary Somalis acted on their own. Still, Giumale tried to control the flow of his attack. Aideed also sent Giumale written orders not to let the Americans escape.

If the Americans had entrenched themselves, then the Somalis would have a difficult time trying to dig them out. Giumale had many fighters, but he had taken massive casualties during attacks on TFR positions and from the AH-6s. Like the Americans, he was under some time pressure too. The Americans and UN would not let their forces stay surrounded. A rescue attempt could occur at any time. Once daylight broke, UNOSOM II's tanks, additional helicopters, and more soldiers could free TFR.

Giumale thought that he could use 60mm mortars to displace the Americans. Complaints and pleas from Mogadishu residents, however, stirred up a debate. The Americans had sensors capable of detecting the source of mortar fire. Attack helicopters would most likely respond quickly to this threat with fire that would destroy nearby homes and create more civilian casualties. Giumale decided not to use the mortars, and later Aideed agreed with his decision. The SNA warlord had built up trust among his clan and he needed to ensure that they continued to support him. Aideed had told his clan and the rest of Mogadishu's population that the UN and the American intention was to convert forcibly the Muslim clans to Christianity and destroy them as a people. The SNA had to appear on the side of the people. Still, his decision to confront the Americans on this Sunday had caused large-scale casualties among SNA militia, irregulars, and non-combatants. American firepower compensated for the Somali numerical superiority.

The Delta soldiers near Super 61 wanted Steele to move forward to consolidate their positions. Steele's Rangers would provide extra firepower to the relatively small force at the MH-60. With the increasing numbers of wounded at the CCP, defending the crash site was getting tough. Despite the need to move together, Steele would not budge. He too had wounded and moving at night, without night vision, might produce even more casualties from the concentrated Somali fire. With his wounded Rangers, Steele could do little but watch them and hope for rescue. He pressed the TFR JOC to get the QRF moving, or else they would have more dead Americans.

Confusion on National Street

A few minutes after the rescue force left the New Port, the convoy started to attract Somali attention. As the convoy passed the last Pakistani-held checkpoint, the tanks let the Malaysians take the lead. The two lead Malaysian Condors started to receive heavy fire as they moved west onto National Street. RPGs and gunfire rocked the Condors, causing their drivers to separate from the convoy. David was in his command HMMWV, the third vehicle in the column, and could only watch as the Condors drove away.

The Condors contained elements of Company A's 2nd Platoon. By coincidence, the two Condors turned left onto a street that passed Durant's

The QRF rescue effort would include units such as this UNITAF psychological operations detachment. Although the Psyops personnel were not required to transmit loudspeaker messages, their use as reinforcements to rescue TFR was a big help in supplementing the force. (DoD)

crashed Black Hawk. Under constant fire, the Malaysian drivers did not stop, but drove down the block. An RPG hit the first Condor, killing the driver. The second vehicle took a RPG round that struck its engine compartment. The platoon leader directed his soldiers to establish security around the area. From the first and second vehicle, soldiers created a perimeter on a street corner near a walled building. The remaining soldiers, including the platoon leader, created another position near a garage. Eventually, the groups consolidated their perimeter near the destroyed lead Condor.

Unfortunately, the Americans and Malaysians were on their own. No other vehicles from the rescue column followed down the road – the rest of the column moved toward the Olympic Hotel. The group would create an assembly point where the Pakistani ex-NATO M48s and some of the APCs would secure the route back for everyone to their stadium base camp. The Condors and HMMWVs would advance into the Black Sea area toward Super 61 while Company C would move to Super 64. After numerous attempts at trying to contact David, the elements of the separated platoon finally reached the battalion commander only after removing some secure communications devices. They were told to remain in position; Americans were about half a mile away. Unfortunately, the surrounded 2nd Platoon had to wait. Despite trying to establish a defensive position, the Somalis peppered the group with gunfire and RPGs. They had to move.

Company C soldiers had advanced toward the crash site by 0210hrs. They were only about a block away from the 2nd Platoon and could hear fire. Somalis started to attack the Americans soon after the US troops had occupied the site at 0227hrs. The rescue force could not determine what had happened to Durant, his crew, Gordon, or Shughart. Delta members did find blood trails, remnants of clothing, and many spent cartridges, but no bodies. Somali interpreters questioned residents, but did not get any more information. There were no responses to the soldiers calling out the names of their missing comrades. After determining there was nothing more to do concerning the missing men, the Delta team that accompanied Company C oversaw the destruction of Super 64 with thermite grenades. The Black Hawk still had classified systems and materials that might fall into Somali hands.

At about 0300hrs, the Company C commander told the separated platoon to move north toward his location. The Somalis had too many forces that blocked Company C from breaking through to the separated platoon. The platoon moved out with the help of AH-1s and now AH-6s; since the 2nd Platoon had been surrounded, the airspace management plan was scrapped for the rescue.

The platoon started to move out toward Company C, while Somali gunmen continued to inflict casualties on the group. A soldier tried to identify the location of Somali gunmen in a building that blocked their way north. The building was marked by an M203 flare, and an AH-6 destroyed it. Unfortunately, the flare was on the wrong building, so the platoon leader contacted the AH-6 again, but used tracer fire from his M16 to mark the target. This time AH-6 minigun fire and rocket rounds demolished the right structure.

OCTOBER 4 1993

0155hrs QRF elements link up

AH-6Js provided close air support day and night to the Rangers and Delta members assigned to Somalia. AH-6J Little Birds skillfully used their 7.62mm miniguns and rocket pods to provide the major fire support to the surrounded Task Force Ranger units in Mogadishu. (DoD)

The 2nd Platoon and Malaysians finally made it to Company C's position. Two Condors took them back to the Pakistani compound. Somalis had killed one American and another died of his wounds, later in a hospital in Germany. Several Malaysians also became casualties in the skirmish. Company C's mission was over.

TFR Gets Out

The Company A commander, Captain Drew Meyerowich, was getting close to the Super 61 location. He had already lost part of his company to the two off-course Condors, but he pushed forward to unite with the TFR forces. He had to endure delays and problems throughout the trip up to National Street. During the journey, the Pakistanis did not want to go forward due to a Somali-built blockade (blockades could mean mines or a possible ambush), and QRF soldiers had to dismount from their vehicles and disassemble it. Malaysian reluctance to move by the Olympic Hotel on Hawlwadig Road also stalled the advance. Taking apart a roadblock here would add time to the rescue mission. Meyerowich's Rangers and the volunteer TFR members decided not to wait and got out of the Condors and HMMWVs at 0036hrs. They would move on foot and let the Condors and other vehicles catch up with them near the crash site later. They were about four blocks away and would have to navigate through Somali-held territory. Fortunately, they were close to the trapped Americans and they had their night-vision goggles. The Condors and other vehicles would follow to pick up the survivors and the dead.

Company A's advance was slow. By 0120hrs, the rescue force picked its way through Somali snipers, several blocks of territory, and obstacles. The rescuers' position was a little more than 300 yards from their objective. SNA militiamen attacked throughout their movement, causing innumerable starts and stops and inflicting further casualties.

Guided by surveillance helicopters, Meyerowich reported to David that he had reached his goal, the TFR perimeter, at 0150hrs, and he linked up with Steele five minutes later. Steele insisted that he was still in charge of the situation on the ground and started to take command of the QRF soldiers. A senior SOF officer, who accompanied the QRF, countermanded Steele, however. Meyerowich had to assess the situation and take account of all personnel. He had about 110 men with him and he created a wider security perimeter to protect the TFR members. This perimeter allowed the disparate TFR elements to gather near the crashed Black Hawk for their recovery.

Attempts throughout the night to free Wolcott's body had all failed. TFR soldiers had tried to cut and pull out his remains without success. They would not leave his remains for the Somalis to desecrate, however. At one point, a

OCTOBER 4
1993

0542hrs
TFR begins
moving out of
crash site

QRF HMMWV tried to pull apart the Black Hawk cockpit to get Wolcott out. While the medics tried to free Wolcott, other Americans removed or destroyed any secure devices and classified materials in the MH-60.

Time was becoming a critical factor, as every delay could mean heavier Somali fire. Soldiers boarded the Condors and HMMWVs with the wounded and dead. Finally, the medics extracted Wolcott's body by 0530hrs. Super 61 was then destroyed in its entirety. The rescue force was getting ready to move out, but had to wait until 0537hrs to depart. The column had 40–50 critical wounded and they needed to get to a medical facility. Unfortunately, there was not enough passenger capacity for all to ride out in the Condors or HMMWVs. Some of the TFR original forces, from Perino's chalk, and Company A soldiers, approximately 15, had to move out on foot with the convoy back to the stadium. They would use the vehicles as mobile shields against enemy fire. In the last few rushed minutes of trying to get out of the area, soldiers attempted to get into the cramped vehicles. Litters took up space and the force needed more Condors or other transportation.

Along the exit route, Pakistani soldiers cleared mines, while Cobras and Little Birds provided cover overhead. The Pakistani tanks fired at buildings where gunfire and RPGs appeared to come from. Unfortunately, operating in a long column with staggered stops and starts, some Condors and other vehicles ended up making a dash to the stadium, leaving some soldiers on foot behind to face Somali gunfire all along the route. After moving about six blocks, Perino flagged down a Pakistani M113 APC and some HMMWVs at 0610hrs. They stopped after some persuasion, and allowed the footslogging soldiers to get aboard the M113. The Rangers crammed inside, and moved off at 0620hrs. Ten minutes later, the convoy reached the safety of the Pakistani base and a field medical hospital set up for the wounded. Some of the HMMWVs returned to the New Port area.

Reports listed all personnel accounted for except for Durant's missing crew and the two snipers. The 14-hour mission was finally over. The ultimately tally was 18 Americans and one Malaysian dead. Eighty-four Americans and seven Malaysians suffered wounds. An unknown number of Somalis died – estimates range from 300 to 500 killed and 700 to 1,000 wounded. Due to the primitive medical support and unsanitary living conditions, many Somali wounded who would have recovered probably died afterwards from infection and neglect.

Two days later on, on October 6, a Somali mortar attack on the airfield killed a TFR soldier and wounded 16 others. Those were the final casualties of TFR's Somali deployment. The force never conducted another raid again.

UN forces used M113 APCs in Somalia. A Pakistani-operated M113 picked up several TFR members, who had to move on foot out of the crash site. Once at the Pakistani base, TFR arranged for medical aid and transportation back to the airport. (DoD)

OCTOBER 4
1993

0630hrs
QRF and TRF
survivors arrive
at Pakistani base
with TFR

ANALYSIS

The battle of Mogadishu was a watershed event for Washington. Despite overwhelming odds, TFR survived a harrowing mission. The Americans' spirited defense and actions resulted in a tactical victory, with a large number of Somali casualties and the successful capture of 24 SNA personnel. Aideed and the SNA suffered tremendous punishment, and some TFR and UN officers believed that the SNA would have crumbled if the Americans had struck again.

Yet the battle was a costly victory, with many Americans killed and wounded. Horrified by the carnage, the American public and Congress quickly turned against Clinton's policy in Somalia. Amongst the most poignant scenes from Mogadishu was the mistreatment of American dead and of Durant at the hands of the SNA and Mogadishu residents. Many Americans expressed outrage, especially as US forces had been helping to avert Somali famine. Clinton quickly announced, on October 7, America's withdrawal from Somalia by March 31, 1994. The President also ordered TFR to leave Somalia; it departed Mogadishu on October 25.

The US retreat handed Aideed what he most wanted, as after the Americans left the UN would soon follow. The SNA claimed a strategic victory. This situation appeared similar to that of the 1968 Tet Offensive in South Vietnam, in which the Viet Cong had suffered tremendous losses but Washington, stung by a strategic surprise, began plans to curtail its involvement in the war and turn to a negotiated settlement. The Mogadishu fight would not only have immediate effects in Somalia, but affect future US involvement in Africa. Some critics argue that Washington's reluctance to get drawn into further African civil wars, like Rwanda, was due partly to Mogadishu.

Mogadishu offers several lessons in fighting a guerilla force in an urban environment. One of the major problems facing the Americans was trying to accomplish unclear political objectives using military means. The initial UN goal was to feed Somalis, but the objective then changed to securing and finally rebuilding Somalia. Once the UN announced a reward for Aideed's capture, the chance for a political settlement was greatly diminished. Trying to weaken and isolate Aideed and his supporters only seemed to create more friction between

Somalis and the UN and exacerbated the situation. If the UN captured Aideed, would not another clan or warlord take control over Somalia?

American forces had a technological advantage over the SNA. Still, technology alone could not trump a wily and dedicated foe. Helicopters provided speed and surprise at decisive points. Although they were an integral part of TFR, the helicopter also became an Achilles heel when their loss forced a change of mission from raid to rescue. Without a means to extract the downed crews, American and UN forces had to fight to save and recover TFR.

Surprise was a key element for success in the TFR raids. Unfortunately, the location of TFR, at the airport, allowed many Somali contractors and observers to witness activities that could tip off the SNA on pending operations. A potential lapse in operational security allowed SNA operatives to alert the militia throughout the city. Similarly, the repeated use of templates for planning allowed the Somalis to create countermeasures to the Americans, such as using RPGs as surface-to-air missiles against the helicopters. The reward on Aideed also telegraphed the UN's intention to widen the conflict. TFR's arrival confirmed this view to the Somalis, as it was the means to accomplish Aideed's capture. TFR also used its ability to operate at night to accomplish most of its previous raids. Unfortunately, it had to respond to what the situation dictated, and the October 3 mission was launched in daylight, negating TFR's ability to surprise the Black Sea residents and the advantages of night operations.

Much confusion surrounding the TFR operations involved issues of unity of command. The UNOSOM II forces had a chain of command to Bir; Garrison reported directly to CENTCOM and bypassed the UN. Garrison could act independently of the UN and was not obligated to follow their directives. He did inform both the UN and Montgomery of certain operations, but only with the minimum of information. Montgomery nominally worked for Bir, but he also had command of the US Forces Somalia. Montgomery, like Garrison, reported to CENTCOM under this command arrangement. Although Garrison and Montgomery worked under the same headquarters, long-range unified planning was limited. Many efforts within the organizations had duplicated missions. The lack of a timely response to rescue TFR may, in part, have been the result of a divided chain of command. Additionally, Howe and the TFR seemed to work independently. Coordinated efforts to solve the clan problems appeared limited.

There were many unknown mission variables. Some of these variables – like inconsistent intelligence, unknown levels of opposition, technical malfunctions, units getting lost, accidents, and other incidents – could lead to mission failure. Despite these factors, TFR used only two templates. Using the strongpoint or convoy templates simplified the mission planning, but also constrained options for the commander. In addition, mission contingencies were restricted to the CSAR helicopter for immediate response and an on-call capability from the QRF and UN. Although these forces were well equipped, they had to face hundreds of armed Aideed supporters. AH-1 and AH-6 attack helicopters did provide some fire-support flexibility, but they also had limited firepower and numbers. Aspin's decision to withhold AC-130s, tanks, and APCs inhibited Garrison's options. Somalis feared the AC-130s, with their

OCTOBER 7 1993

President Clinton orders US troops' withdrawal

long loiter times, night vision and massive firepower. M1 Abrams tanks and M2 Bradleys could have broken through to the crash sites faster and with fewer casualties than the HMMWVs and trucks. There has been much debate and controversy over the denial of requests for these weapons.

The Pentagon's desire to keep the force in Somalia small, while conducting actual military operations, seemed contradictory. Under UNITAF, the United States contributed two divisions and many support forces to conduct peacekeeping operations. The only American combat forces available in October were TFR and the QRF to raid and strike against one of the most powerful clans in Somalia. Under UNITAF, the Army and Marine Corps units could intimidate the clans. The UNOSOM II forces did not have the same impact as the American UNITAF forces, which conducted continual sweeps and checkpoint security around the city. TFR and the QRF could not provide the same level of presence nor reaction to the SNA as UNITAF. Unless Washington provided overwhelming military force, TFR/QRF operations ran a greater risk of failure.

Overconfidence in TFR capabilities also played a part in the problems during the raid. Many Rangers believed that the raid would not last long and would encounter little opposition. They had conducted similar raids in the past and this particular mission seemed like a repeat of the previous efforts, except now the location was in the heart of Aideed-controlled territory and in daylight. Soldiers did not take water, they modified equipment loads, and left behind night-vision goggles. Pilots acknowledged the Black Hawk helicopter destruction a week earlier, but they largely ignored this key event until the downing of Super 61. Repeated American templates also demonstrated the lack of awareness of Somali abilities to adapt to those tactics. Aideed correctly positioned forces to force down a helicopter and he knew the Americans would attempt to rescue its endangered crew. From there, he could surround the crew and their rescue forces and destroy it while other SNA fighters blocked any reinforcements. Unfortunately, many Americans planners did not believe the Somalis could organize and execute such an operation.

Once Wolcott's helicopter was down, the Somalis altered the mission's nature. TFR plans and actions had focused on swift offensive actions. The Americans exercised their ability to select their targets and strike at areas of weakness against a superior force. Once they took a prisoner or raided a facility, they could quickly leave. On October 3, the Rangers and Delta members faced a different conflict; they were now on the defensive and did not hold the initiative against the Somalis. The fight became a slugging match in which the SNA supporters were willing to sacrifice many to kill Americans. This attritional battle was a consequence not envisaged in the TFR plans. Fortunately, Super 66's resupply effort and the QRF and UN relief column averted a potential disaster for the Americans.

Although TFR and other Americans had conducted orientation trips to Somalia before deployment, and the soldiers did have introductory courses on the area, the US troops still had difficulty understanding the environment in which they operated. Inter-clan warfare, urban fighting, harsh African conditions, working with the UN and NGOs, and other environmental factors affected TFR. Understanding the people of Somalia and gaining their trust, especially when TFR relied on HUMINT, was critical to success. Perhaps using other clans against the Habr Gidr, improved intelligence, psychological operations, diplomacy, and more sophisticated military means could indeed have stifled Aideed. Trying to fight an enemy who did not wear a uniform or distinctive insignia, and who could blend into the local environment, was frustrating to the UN troops and the Americans, especially in a dense urban environment like Mogadishu. Although the Americans tried to avoid unnecessary fire, combat operations often resulted in civilian casualties. These casualties contributed to further hatred of TFR and added more fighters to Aideed's side.

American casualties brought immediate, intense aversion from the American public. Somalia was not a vital national interest for Washington. The public had lost interest in the Somali mission and most US citizens were unaware of the change from humanitarian famine relief to nation building. In the course of a year, Americans had turned from transporting food to conducting military operations. Mission creep expanded America's role, but Washington seemed unsure of a desired end state for Somalia. Given the ambiguous mission in Mogadishu and 18 deaths, the immediate demand for withdrawal seemed a logical conclusion.

Aideed was very adept at using his limited resources to combat the Americans and the UN. He aimed at the one center of gravity that would alter the conflict – the American public. Raising the level of violence, demonstrating a willingness and ability to fight a prolonged war, and the skillful manipulation of the media allowed Aideed to turn the tables on Washington. He made rebuilding Somalia too costly for the Americans. Any peace efforts would have to come through him. American technology and superior firepower did not automatically translate into victory. Like all conflicts, the results came down to which side implemented the best strategy.

If there was a bright spot for the Americans, it was the TFR and QFR adaptability to adjust to a fluid situation and avert a major catastrophe. Small-unit leadership and tactics worked relatively well in the defensive positions throughout the night of the battle. American actions proved Somali clan assumptions wrong when they questioned the Americans' determination to fight while taking casualties. TFR and QRF forces continued to mount relief columns into the most deadly parts of Mogadishu to relieve their surrounded comrades. The Little Bird crews flew into the heart of Somali opposition to prevent it from overwhelming the forces at Super 61, despite anti-helicopter RPG fire.

The battle of Mogadishu provides a good case study of future crises in failed states. Despite using specially trained SOF, the Americans faced many problems trying to find and capture Aideed, problems that they would repeat a decade later in Iraq and Afghanistan. Irregular warfare, an anonymous foe, ambiguous strategy, operating in a complex tribal state, and conflicting political objectives have become common factors in today's conflicts much like Somalia in 1993.

CONCLUSION

By 1992, Washington had come to Somalia to solve famine and civil unrest in a demonstration of US post-Cold War confidence. Yet operating in a failed state proved a tougher challenge than envisaged. The mission expanded into an unending fight between UN personnel and Somali clans, both vying for control over a war-torn region. After the Mogadishu raid, America withdrew largely from Africa and became more skeptical of direct involvement in unstable nations. The fight for Mogadishu literally changed American foreign policy, especially in Africa, for years.

Despite TFR's eventual tactical victory, the raid on October 3, 1993, was a strategic failure. Once the SNA adapted to the American tactics, the Somalis almost destroyed the Super 61 rescue force. Technologically advanced weapons could not overcome some of the serious issues from

After the action of October 3–4, Washington did not want a repeat of the battle of Mogadishu casualties. The Pentagon approved added troops, APCs, and tanks, like this M1A1, from the 24th Infantry Division to protect the American force in Somalia and subdue the clans. (DoD)

which TFR suffered. The loss of surprise, security problems, and other issues, coupled with the Somalis' waging of an asymmetric campaign, overcame the American ability to respond quickly and strike with impunity. Aideed's change in strategy caught TFR's SOF in a desperate situation. Fortunately, the leadership and training of US forces proved their worth and saved them from an overwhelming defeat.

The battle of Mogadishu was an example of future problems that Washington would face fighting clans or irregular forces in cities. The American military did not want to become involved in nation-building efforts that they were not trained, organized, or equipped to accomplish. Washington had to recognize its limit of power, especially after losing its political will to continue operating in Somalia. Vague political objectives and flawed decisions created the conditions that ultimately defeated America's mission in Somalia. The loss of resolve to remain in Mogadishu forced the UN to negotiate with Aideed after America's announced withdrawal from the region. Aideed declared himself president, but this claim did not unify Somalia. Others vied for control. Aideed stayed in

power until he died of a gunshot wound in 1996. Curiously, the SNA named his son as the president. His son had emigrated to the United States and had become an American citizen. He even served as a US Marine in UNITAF. He later resigned as president in an attempt to create a new government for Somalia, but the move failed.

Somalia continued as a failed state for years. Although the people of Somalia elected a coalition government, it could not stop the country becoming a hotbed for training and raising Islamic terrorists, and Islamic leaders took control of southern Somalia. Fighting between clans continues today and economic failure still sweeps the land. Somalia's main economic activities are criminal ones, including piracy. Crime and terrorism threaten the stability of the neighboring nations. The problems that the US forces attempted to solve back in 1993 have, sadly, continued to this day, with little sign of abating.

Despite the massive effort to help Somalia, the country fell into civil war. Today, the country still has clan and religious factions that vie for power. Their conflict has also spread to neighboring countries and the people continue to suffer. Piracy has become an industry along the coastal areas. (DoD).

BIBLIOGRAPHY

Atkinson, Rick, "Night of a Thousand Casualties: Firefight in Mogadishu – the Last Mission of Task Force Ranger Series 2/2," *Washington Post* (January 31, 1994, A-01)

Atkinson, Rick, "The Raid That Went Wrong: How an Elite US Force Failed in Somalia: Firefight in Mogadishu – the Last Mission of Task Force Ranger Series 1/2," *Washington Post* (January 30, 1994, A-01)

Bahmanyar, Mir, *Shadow Warriors: A History of the US Army Rangers*, Osprey Publishing, Oxford, (2005)

Baumann, Robert F. (ed.), *My Clan against the World: US and Coalition Forces in Somalia 1992–1994*, Combat Studies Institute Press, Fort Leavenworth, KS (undated)

Bowden, Mark, *Black Hawk Down: A Story of Modern War*, Signet, New York (2002)

Davidson, Ronald H., Personal Experience Monograph, *Somalia: One Soldier's Experience*, US Army War College, Carlisle Barracks, PA (1998)

Delong, Kent and Steve Tuckey, *Mogadishu! Heroism and Tragedy*, Praeger, Westport, CT (1994)

Di Tomasso, Thomas, *The Battle of the Black Sea, Bravo Company, 3rd Ranger Battalion, 75th Ranger Regiment, 3–4 Oct 1993*, US Infantry School, Infantry Officer Advanced Course 4-94, Fort Benning, GA

Eckland, Marshall V., "Analysis of Operation Gothic Serpent," *Special Warfare*, Vol. 16, Issue 4 (May 2004)

Eckland, Marshall V., "Task Force Ranger vs. Urban Somali Guerillas in Mogadishu: An Analysis on Guerilla and Counter Guerilla Tactics and Techniques used during Operation *Gothic Serpent*," *Small Wars and Insurgencies*, Vol. 15, No. 3 (Winter 2004)

Eversmann, Matt and Dan Schilling (eds), *The Battle of Mogadishu: Firsthand Accounts from the Men of the Task Force Ranger*, Ballantine Books, New York (2005)

Fast, James T., Personal Experience Monograph, *Task Force Ranger in Somalia Isaiah 6:8*, US Army War College, Carlisle Barracks, PA (1999)

Ferry, Charles F., "Personal Account of a Rifle Company XO," *Infantry*, Vol. 84, No. 5 (September/October 1994)

Garrison, William F., *After Action Report: Task Force Ranger Operations in Support of UNOSOM II, 22 August–15 October 1993* (January 5, 1994, declassified)

Hollis, Mark A.B., "Platoon Under Fire: Mogadishu, October 1993" *Infantry*, Vol. 88, No. 1 (January–April 1998)

Sangvic, Roger N., *Battle of Mogadishu: Anatomy of a Failure*, School of Advanced Military Studies, Fort Leavenworth, KS (December 16, 1998)

Stewart, Richard, *The United States Army in Somalia 1992–1994*, Center of Military History, Washington, DC (2002)

Tovy, Tal, "Are the Principles of War Applicable to Special Forces? Operation *Gothic Serpent* Re-examined," *The RUSI Journal*, Vol. 154, No. 2 (April 2009)

US Army, *United States Forces, Somalia After Action Report and Historical Overview: The United States Army in Somalia, 1992–1994*, Center of Military History, Washington, DC (2003)

US Special Operations Command/US Army Special Operations Command, *Task Force Ranger Operations in Somalia 3–4 October 1993* (June 1, 1994, declassified)

van Drie, Mark, Personal Experience Monograph, *Humanitarian Relief and Hunting Aideed: My Time with the US Army Quick Reaction Force in Somalia*, US Army War College, Carlisle Barracks, PA (2000)

Warner, John and Carl Levin, *Review of the Circumstances Surrounding the Ranger Raid on October 3–4, 1993 in Mogadishu, Somalia*, US Congress, Senate, Committee on Armed Services, Washington, DC (September 29, 1995)

Weiss, Jack, Personal Experience Monograph, *Supporting the Quick Reaction Force in Somalia: Operation Continue Hope/Somalia*, US Army War College, Carlisle Barracks, PA (1996)

INDEX